HIJACKING REALITY

The Reprogramming
& Reorganization
of Human Life

KINGSLEY L. DENNIS

Beautiful Traitor Books

Copyright © 2021 by Kingsley L. Dennis

All rights reserved. No part of this work may be reproduced or transmitted in any form or by any means, electronic or mechanical, including photocopying and recording, or by any information storage or retrieval system without the prior written permission of Beautiful Traitor Books.

Published by Beautiful Traitor Books –
http://www.beautifultraitorbooks.com/

Any person who does any unauthorized act in relation to this publication may be liable to criminal prosecution and civil claims for damages. The author has asserted his right to be identified as the author of this work in accordance with the Copyright, Design and Patents Act 1988.

ISBN-13: 978-1-913816-22-3 (paperback)

First Edition: 2021

Cover Concept: Kingsley L. Dennis & Ibolya Kapta

Cover Design: Ibolya Kapta

Cover photo: Neon City Street at Night

by Well Naves

Copyright 2021 by Beautiful Traitor Books.

All rights reserved.

info@beautifultraitorbooks.com

CONTENTS

Introduction Mutating Realities   1

PART ONE
The Collapse of Consensus

One	A Consensus Reality Meltdown	11
Two	A Failure of Perception	20
Three	Prophesizing Media (or Predictive Programming?)	29
Four	Hyperreality (or Mutation?)	38
Five	Entering the Void	46

PART TWO
The Resetting of New Narratives

Six	Defragmenting the Mind	55
Seven	The New Reign of Biopower	64

Eight	Biosecurity: the biology of control	76
Nine	Psycho-Power	85
Ten	Unfreedom Narratives: the new states of exception	92
Eleven	New Landscapes: the *organization* of behaviour modification	101

PART THREE

Bodily Futures

Twelve	Weak Bodies	113
Thirteen	Neuro-Techno Totalitarianism	122
Fourteen	The New Nihilism - a cult of the irrational?	131
Fifteen	Rise of the Heretics	139

| **Afterword** | 153 |
| **References** | 156 |

INTRODUCTION

Mutating Realities

*'Better the demon which makes you improve
than the angel who threatens.'*
Idries Shah, *Caravan of Dreams*

There is an advancing 'irrationality' in our age, and it may either entrap us or be our way of escape from the *iron cage* of the rational. Perhaps it is this irrationality that is behind the encroaching sense of nihilism as our global human civilization enters a grand mutation, or transition. The question, however, is who or what is directing this mutation as it advances? Mutational moments, in history as well as in biology, are delicate and vulnerable times for they are open to receiving the malicious, or bad intentions, as well as the beneficial influences. As the world renown biologist Edward Wilson wrote: 'The problem before us is how to feed billions of new mouths over the next several decades and save the rest of life at the same time, without being wrapped in a Faustian bargain that threatens freedom and security. No one knows the exact solution to this dilemma.'[1] He would not be alone in thinking these thoughts. And perhaps some people did come up with a solution – only that, it *did* come 'wrapped in a Faustian bargain that threatens freedom and security.' What if the upheavals now being witnessed across the world – from the pandemic, failing economies, increased surveillance, biosecurity, digitization, rapid automation, and the rest - are part of an overall plan to remake the world in a new image? An image to suit a certain sector of our societies. Perhaps, for the first time in modern history, a relatively small group of people are attempting to establish a secular consensus reality (worldview) upon a global scale. Would that even be possible?

Modern life has been compared to the 'Theatre of the Absurd' (yet by whom, I do not recall). Human reality is malleable because it lacks any Absolutes. To use a known analogy, human life is a series of programs within programs. For many people still, the only reality is the reality of *this world*. In and of itself, this is a major limitation. The many-sided complexities of life are often presented as grand simplifications by the zealous materialists. Grand ideologies have scoured the Earth, reaping adherents and proselytizers. Such sweeping narratives became the giant beasts of Truth; they also became the backdrop for multiple wars and mutilations. People were fed and weaned on gargantuan myths, narratives, and historical agendas. The colossal pillars of 'Truth' in its time became the founding blocks of many nations, peoples, and cultural groupings. We have become used to *living our lives according to the beliefs we behold*.

The void of internal distrust, uncertainty, and doubt was often filled from the cup of external influences and propagandized truths. Stories, myths, and narratives have always been the tapestry of the human life. It is from these that we have played our games – from the civilizational to the individual. Stories and narratives are there to appease and ease our human restlessness. For when we are restless, we show signs of psychological disorientation.

This is the retrograde moment we are each experiencing in our own ways. It may be said, as some have, that humanity is experiencing its period of 'Modern Nihilism' where unpleasant excesses and perspectives are being expunged into the public sphere. Along with this, it seems that our individual and collective memory of the past is continually changing – mutating into neo-memories that replace the existing ones and become the new host. Each in our way, we are losing hold onto our collective past and in its place is arising an incoherency. No one is sharing the same space anymore. If we cannot agree over what is the 'same' then we creep ever closer to the 'insane.' This is the realm of absurdity where there is no agreed-upon stability or shared reference points. We each become adrift upon a sea of our own endlessly mutating swarm of neo-memories. The past becomes like a retrospective art installation and we are the voyeurs.

What is the state of the collective psychosphere of our times? This is what I am trying to delve into through the pages of this book. Maybe we shall find that Lady Reason is packing her bags and leaving us and, in her place, we shall discover the Mad Professor of Myth and Magic has stepped in? It is the same chair they occupy, but the outlook is as far apart as can be imagined. John Maynard Keynes is said to have written somewhere that the unavoidable does not generally happen because the unpredictable prevails. And so, where does this leave us – looking in the eyes of the unavoidable whilst waiting for the surprise visit of the unpredictable?

Maybe this leaves us somewhere within the opening phases of the largest psychological exercise in the history of humanity. Now, that sounds dramatic. Yet we really need to take a look at what is currently going on in the world. We are seeing and hearing many things, but I am not sure that we are critically perceiving the many layers in operation. What if I propose that what many of us are presently experiencing is the process of a monumental mind programming operation? If 'Operation Mind Control'[i] was not already a title of a well-known book, then I would propose that title here. Prior to 2020, people were more or less entrained or 'locked in' to their rhythms of familiarity. The pathways and contours of everyday life were relatively known and mapped for most people, especially those living in industrialized, developed societies. Then 2020 happened – and the unpredictable arrived on our doorsteps. The world was thrown into a great 'halt' – we literally came to a global stop. Locally, and across the world, humanity has entered a huge experiment. For the first time in our known history, human civilization in most of its forms has come to a halt. We have been stopped in mid-posture – *a state of arrested movement* - and have been placed in a space we are totally unaccustomed to. Have we not just experienced a 'stop' command enforced upon us globally with the array of national lockdowns and the halt of global travel, trade, and mobility? Such a sudden 'stop' to our familiar, conditioned movement and behaviour is almost a way of 'breaking open the head,' such as used also in both mind programming and behaviour modification processes. It all depends on what comes after the sudden stop – is it a moment for critical reflection and observation, or an implant of fear and uncertainty? For many people around the world, the sudden rise of local and national quarantines, lockdowns, and restriction of mobilities, coupled with the new security laws and rules on mask-wearing and social distancing, have created an atmosphere and energy of fear, uncertainty, instability, and even panic and paranoia. The human collective psyche was 'cracked open' and then almost simultaneously fed with inputs that further destabilized it and created various levels of dissonance. Never before has this occurred, nor has it been possible. This has certainly created a great deal of anxiety, depression, anger, revolt, and increased suicides across the world, as is evidenced by both the numbers and the physical scenes. There has likewise been a breaking down of social alliances, friendships, and family bonds, due to con-

---

i   *Operation Mind Control* by Walter Bowart (1978)

flicting beliefs and opinions. Social and personal identities – the 'sense of self' – have come under scrutiny as cultural and racial tensions rise. To a degree, a de-fragmenting of the human self has occurred. And this is also the same process used in mind-programming – or brainwashing – a person. First, a person's coherent viewpoint, their stability of mind, is broken down until a deep level of cognitive dissonance occurs. And within this state of vulnerability, a new narrative is introduced that gives the person a feeling of regaining stability. We may ask: has a huge, global deconditioning process been put into operation? That is, people are being dis-connected from their links to the familiar in order to re-program them with a new reality – a 'new normal' – that is relatable to the new social-political power structures.

A coherent world requires a coherent and shared worldview – a consensus reality paradigm. For a civilization to be successful, its citizens must largely agree upon a shared reality consensus. For a global civilization to be stable and sustainable, it too must share a coherent consensus view of reality, in the majority case. Therefore, in order to engineer a future global civilization, a consensus 'reality paradigm' must likewise be socially managed (and, if necessary, manipulated). This is what this book is about. I propose that there are major powerful players upon this planet that wish to steer humanity into a global civilization. Their thinking is that it was likely to happen at some point, so why not take the upper hand and steer it into place? At least this way, those that jump to take the helm can at least steer it in a direction that benefits their aims. And, of course, when you have almost eight billion people upon the planet, then that is a lot of people to convince to your aims. Yet, what if instead of trying to force the issue, you can make people *believe* in the story themselves? That way, they will agree that it is the worldview for them and adhere to it willingly. To get people on board with an idea, the most effective way is to 'implant' the idea into them so that it feels like it is homegrown. Many people do this all the time, through acts of persuasion – or, in extreme cases, through hypnosis. In a way, getting a group of people to change their minds is a form of hypnosis. On a larger scale, this can be viewed as cultural hypnosis. On a worldwide scale - well, this has not been attempted before. Maybe this is what we are witnessing now?

     Many populations are currently within the throes of a 'global mind change' yet are unaware of this. They are unaware of the set of processes that are attempting to install a new 'paradigm thinking chip' which is based on the slogan of the 'new normal.' Yet, as in all transition moments, things can go in more than one direction. As well as a solidification or crystallization into a new mindset, there can also be a 're-calibration' into an unexpected phase. This global moment of psychological disruption and fragmenting through de-conditioning can also tip into a breakthrough to a new state of mind and perception. This de-layering process, or stripping away, can take people down to their essential self; yet, instead of a new program, or narrative, being installed, it may also trigger a 'jump moment' into completely new and unheralded consciousness patterns. I contend that we are now moving into a monumental 'choice moment,' and we may be compelled to ask ourselves – *what does it mean to be human?*

This book is a survey of these processes that are playing out right now across the world and which are attempting to influence collective human reality. I invite you to join me on this tour. To begin with, we should start out with looking at how our consensus reality has been brought into collapse. Here we go. Ready? ...

PART ONE

The Collapse of Consensus

ONE

A Consensus Reality Meltdown

'False clarity is only another name for myth.'

Adorno & Horkheimer - *Dialectic of Enlightenment*

'Consensus reality is the ultimate secret society. It is a society so secret that even its members are unaware of its existence.'

Jason Horsley

The year 2020 will go down in the history books as an unforgettable year. No-one could have foretold what was going to unfold, or just how almost every aspect of our lives was going to be affected. Yet the signs were there. People had been writing about the 'transition' tipping points for a number of years, and many fellow commentators all sensed that something was coming – we just were not sure *how* it would arrive.

In December 2019 I was asked by the editor of an Australian magazine[i] to produce a short commentary for the year 2020. This was perhaps the third time I had done so, and I was expected to give my speculations (forecast) for what I considered may likely be the outlook for the coming twelve months. I wrote my piece and emailed it off in December, in time for the January 2020 issue. It was titled 'Year

---

i   New Dawn magazine

Ahead 2020: Consensus Reality Meltdown.' For some reason, the notion of a 'consensus reality meltdown' had come to me when considering the year ahead. I began the short essay by saying that the year ahead into 2020 will continue a process that has already begun and which we are seeing unfolding around us across the globe. I stated that many of us are asking – 'Is reality broken?' And I concluded by saying – 'It almost seems so.'

For many years now, our sense of collective reality has been gradually retreating behind a spectacle of pseudo-events, false news, commercial extremes (e.g., 'Black Fridays'), and a whole host of surface phenomena that creates a shimmering façade of the make-believe. As part of this reality meltdown, I said that the signs and signals that once stood as our guideposts are losing their meaning and becoming indistinguishable from false realities. Here I quoted from sociologist Jean Baudrillard who aptly phrased it as - *The attraction of the void is irresistible.* It is this increasing void that has attracted and continues to attract so many. It is the acceleration of the void that suggests a meltdown of our consensus reality is in process.

The 'objects' or values that we have attempted to live by, or that we pursue - such as power, truth, understanding, dreams, work, love, and the rest - have all seemingly vanished into some elusive realm where the presence of these things no longer tangibly exist. However, the doubt, uncertainty, and the anxiety of their absence – or 'fake presence' – are indeed real enough to affect us deeply. We seek the substitutes for what has already disappeared. We are now cut-off from our own image, adrift on the digital sea. Those markers of our differences and contradictions have further blurred. Their edges now seem smooth rather than jagged. It is no longer the jagged pill we are forced to swallow, but the smooth pill we are willing to pop. The chimera of the real is lining the sides of the rabbit hole of the consensus reality meltdown. As Baudrillard also says – 'Were it not for appearances, the world would be a perfect crime...'[1]

We protect ourselves with the illusion of truth, and the great riddle of our lives is the material illusion that we abide by. Everything withdraws behind its own appearance, so that things appear to take place even when they do not. This is the great absence in our lives - excuses riddled in illusion, hiding through false appearance. We are left to decipher the world, to try and pull back the illusionary curtains. The image has taken the place of the real and robbed it of its role. And behind the image, something has had to disappear. We have been persuaded that the image is better for us, better for our well-being, so that we don't notice when the 'real' quietly slips away unnoticed like an early party-leaver. The world exists as if in a play of appearances; and the crime of life is its incompleteness - a living incompleteness that gnaws at us.

I also wrote in my 'Year Ahead 2020' commentary that in such times when once guiding reality structures begin to break down, manipulative forces become stronger, more pervasive. Such external forces become more involved with our subjective experience of the world. They try to bend our subjective experience to fit a new reshuffling of reality. This is what creates the instabilities, the uncertainties, and the anxiety. A common response to this emerging world would be to strengthen an acceptance of it and thus 'normalize' it. The alternative is to place oneself outside or on the periphery of the system – making one a surveillance target. To live upon the margins may now become the choice of the new conscious objectors. To put it simply, the furthering of the consensus reality meltdown can be described as the normalization of delusion. When mass society adheres to a collective delusion, we come to call it normal – the 'new reality.' And if a person strays too far from this consensus thinking then we often label them as delusional, or unstable. The control and manipulation of human perception is the new battleground. In times as these it is almost inevitable that we are likely to see an increased interest/intervention into 'psychic states' through such institutions as state management, propaganda, entertainment/consumerism, the military, etc. During the meltdown phase and during the transition to a new 'reality-set,' or collective psyche, many players are vying for controlling interests. What we have come to regard as 'reality' will officially become intangible and fluid, leading to the rise of adverse belief-sets such as revised fascist ideologies and revamped left-right politics. We are increasingly losing our bearings, our fixed moorings, and this is likely to lead to further anxiety as people try to cling to invested beliefs. As this continues, many people will inevitably experience discomfort in one form or another.

The blurriness that surrounds us today is breaking up our known terrains and familiar patterns. It is taking apart almost all of what we took to be *our* territories and is re-arranging them. The sacred totems that signified our social realities for so long are now being dismantled. Everyday life is being targeted for the bombardment of the artificial, the *heist* against human cognition. It is a monumental shift away from authenticity and into the manufactured – the manufactured landscapes of a constructed narrative. History has a habit of trying to retain what it believes to be authentic. It tells us that events occurred that were 'authentic events' and these were then recorded – or frozen – for posterity. We grow up among our specific cultural stories and narratives of history, believing that everything happened exactly as recorded. And we also grow up believing that each event starts out as authentic. In literary theory the act of believing the authenticity of a story, even if within us we know it could not have happened the way it is told, is referred to as *the willing suspension of disbelief.* We drop our disbelief in order to allow ourselves to accept the story. Oddly enough, most of us have been doing this for so long that we are accustomed to not questioning our disbelief anymore – rather, we accept everything. The absence of critical disbelief not only feels normal it actually feels comfortable. Yet any reasonable observer has to admit that history is a biased story. It often chooses to tell a certain perspective, depending on where, and by whom, the history is being written. And yet, 'so long as an illusion is not recognized as an error, it has a value precisely equivalent to reality.'[2]

Bodies of authority, political figures, mainstream media channels – virtually all of our significant institutions – have turned, or are in the process of turning, into puppets of propaganda. They serve to produce the *appearance of reality*; yet they fail to represent a *sense of reality* – 'The derealization of the world will be the work of the world itself.'[3] Or, as sci-fi writer Philip K. Dick said in one of his talks:

> We live in a society in which spurious realities are manufactured by the media, by governments, by big corporations, by religious groups, political groups. I ask, in my writing, 'What is real?' Because unceasingly we are bombarded with pseudo realities manufactured by very sophisticated people using very sophisticated electronic mechanisms.[ii]

Philip K. Dick asks what is real as we are under the bombardment and assault of pseudo realities. We may ask ourselves the same question, what is real? Perhaps the perfect crime has been to hide the real so well that our modern societies have ventured beyond the illusion of reality itself. The perfect crime is the perfect cover up. And the cover up has been that a consensus reality meltdown has morphed into the illusion of relative truths.

The Illusion of Relative Truths

Whilst individuals are trying to stay afloat during this meltdown, mainstream institutions are peddling a simplified version of events in order to create the semblance of an appropriate reality. It is an attempt to create a perceptual

••••••••••••••••
ii   Available online from various quote sources, such as - https://www.brainyquote.com/quotes/philip_k_dick_669029

bubble that we are told will explain life for us. After all, too many 'reality events' would only serve to break down this simplified bubble and give us all a headache. And so, a perceptual illusion or simulation is created through the mainstream media and institutions in order to offer a simplified vision of reality. And this simplification involves a world of binaries - the Us vs. Them; Good vs. Bad; Left vs. Right; Truth vs. Conspiracy - and all the rest of these manufactured dichotomies that are brandished as deep truths.

We are witness to a meltdown of various perceptual realities that function as the ether. Each of us are immersed in it even if we are not aware, as fish in the sea do not always debate the water. A globalizing 'thought monster' is arising with the signs and symbols that attempt to define a consensus narrative: health, disease, safety, security, privacy, credit, do 'the right thing,' and all the rest, etc, etc. And many buy into all these terms so deeply that it is no surprise to learn that we are a species in therapy. It seems as if people are being 'educated' to protect themselves with the illusion of relative truths. Everything withdraws behind its own appearance - this is the great absence in our lives. We are left to decipher the world, to try and see through the misty lens of perception. People are left to drift between various narratives as ghosts drift between walls. If everyone believes in a lie, it doesn't stop it from being a lie, or make it into a truth.

It has been said that when a culture, and its people, become unmoored from a consensus reality then they retreat into a world of fantasy. And then this 'fantasy mode' can invert meanings and truths into a whole host of fanciful narratives that feed off trigger words and phrases like *war on terror* or *war on disease*, or *build back better*. When people can no longer distinguish between relative truths, then reality gets usurped and the fantasy world takes over. The meltdown has truly begun. The information and 'news' of today is more about perception and social management than anything else. Influencing minds is more favourable, and more lucrative, than informing them. The end result is both more guaranteed and more controlled. Open information has always been a dangerous thing, as religious and social institutions have long known. Controlled information seeks to create contrived narratives that support specific agendas. As consumers of such narratives, we are accepting and buying into an encroaching unrealism. It is a world of substitution that subverts the mind. It is much easier to confuse and misinform than it is to inculcate opinion. Yet they seem to go hand in hand.

Fake news and alternative facts are further obscuring the veneer of truth by tampering with the already fragile and fragmented sense of reality. The malady of the unreal is spreading like a pandemic. Fake is the new 'new'! The *Oxford English Dictionary* made 'post-truth' its "Word of the Year" in 2016, defining it as 'circumstances in which objective facts are less influential in shaping public opinion than appeals to emotion and personal belief.' With the proliferation of fake news and alternative facts in recent years, the 'fabrication of the fake' has become a core industry within our modern societies. We have become the targeted consumers for stimulated expectations and false desires – 'Advertising is the ubiquitous flow of fake information that systematically models expectations, imagination, subconscious life.'[5] A reflection of the consensus reality meltdown is that there's no longer anything new in fake news. What is the 'new' about it is the speed and intensity; this is what philosopher Franco Berardi refers to as the info-stimulation: 'info-nervous stimulation has intensified beyond the limits of conscious processing.'[6] The social mind of humanity is being increasingly captured by the infosphere that then intensifies info-nervous stimulation. The result is that unconscious forces and energies are being projected externally and manifested in everyday life. The modern world is experiencing a meltdown in consensus reality in part due to an explosion of the human unconscious being projected outwards upon the world. We are collectively living through our fears, anxieties, desires, uncertainties, and traumas without fully realizing what is occurring. And beyond a certain level of intensity, this unconscious assault of nervous stimulations and outpourings becomes an emotional discomfort. The rise of emotional and mental stimulus, along with the rise of the fake and the pseudo, is also causing increased cognitive dissonance (as I discuss later in the book).

Nothing is 'real' in itself but only in relation to other unreal things. The unreality of relative truths is being measured in fractal relation to itself.

Fractal Relations

French philosopher Paul Virilio believes that we have now entered the *acceleration of reality*. He says that in the current era we have reached the limits of instantaneity, the limits of human thought and time. Also, that this era of accelerated reality has led now not to the end of history, as some have wanted us to believe, but to the end of geography.[iii] Virilio says we have polluted our measurement and sense of distance and place, and within this there is a loss of body - a loss of the corporeal. Time, place, and space have become fractalized. That is, our historical sense of continuum, of physical expanse, is being eroded and broken-up into fractals. Yet this is precisely the process required to construct a new perceptual reality narrative. In order to form a new world structure, it is necessary first to dismantle the old narratives that held the old order together. And it isn't only a physical new order but also, importantly, a psychological one. The new reality paradigm or 'world order' must dethrone its imagined enemies to declare a new security state, or world order of security. And this, I contend, is what is occurring now across the world through the attempt at a 'Great Reset.'[iv]

••••••••••••••••••

iii   A reference here to Francis Fukuyama's treatise The End of History

iv   A reference to the World Economic Forum's agenda for global change post-Covid-19

Life has shifted, or been pushed, into a realm of invention and malleability that is being exploited ever more overtly by politicians, mainstream media, and their propaganda machinery. If you feel like you are unsure of what is real and what is unreal then you are not alone. The present life experience is being pushed to the point of abstraction. As a friend once said, it's like a walrus adrift on a sheet of ice. It feels as if we are increasingly facing an absence, and some neo-nihilism is about to raise its head (as I discuss in Part Three). The extreme of this is creating a world where humans feel they are excluded. And with the projected rise of a technologically driven future (as part of the Great Reset), then this is more likely to be the case.

The consensus reality that managed to survive through the past social, cultural, and industrial revolutions has arrived at the point of its own abstraction. Pre-existent fixed identities are losing their meaning and becoming indistinguishable. Fractal relations and the illusion of relative truths have woven a tapestry that is absorbing differences and contradictions and dissolving once-familiar social alliances. And the result is what I refer to as a reality meltdown – or, the failure of perception.

TWO

A Failure of Perception

> *'When a nation becomes unmoored from reality,*
> *it retreats into a world of magic.'*
>
> Chris Hedges, *Empire of Illusion*

Modern life is creeping more and more into a form of abstraction. This has been officially labelled as the 'erosion of the collective perception of objective facts.' I call it the continuation of the consensus reality meltdown – and because of it many people are feeling increasingly distanced from their actions and dumbed to their responsibilities. As the gap between a consensus perception of reality and abstraction widens, people fall into distractions and the 'gameplay.' The English writer Aldous Huxley wrote that 'In *Brave New World* non-stop distractions of the most fascinating nature...are deliberately used as instruments of policy, for the purpose of preventing people from paying too much attention to the realities of their social and political situation.' Huxley feared that people would be rendered passive through access to a plentiful supply of entertainment, consumerism, and a multitude of intoxications. Reality, after all, is a matter of perception. When perceptions are manipulated, overly focused through the intellect, or fall into extreme individualism, then a collective consensus begins to break down – as is happening now. This failure of perception is coinciding with the rise of hyperreality.[i]

The original notion of hyperreality (a term borrowed from semiotics and postmodern theory) is an inability of consciousness to distinguish reality from a simulation of reality, especially in technologically advanced societies. We are no longer faced with the threat of struggling with our shadows – we are now faced with the threat of our clones. This may be the radical illusion we are slipping into through our failure of perception.

Yet the meltdown of reality, or the rise of illusion within the world, has been faced by all cultures. It has been described by mystics, symbolized by art, and struggled over by philosophers. The notion of illusion is not the main issue – rather, it is the medium through which it is conveyed. Or, more importantly, whether it is deliberately exaggerated and amplified. And how, by who – and why? The play of reality (the management of illusion, or hyperreality) is now perhaps the greatest industry within modern society. Hyperreality plays a somewhat different game from a consensus reality – it has new rules and a different deck of cards. The paradox today is that those people caught up in the 'game' have no, or little, idea what the gameplay is. The result is a distortion of how we see things. In other words, a *perception distortion*. To put it simply, hyperreality can be described as the normalization of delusion. When mass society adheres to a collective delusion, we call it normal, or 'reality,' and if one person strays too far from this consensus thinking then they often get labelled as delusional, or unstable. Hyperreality also reflects a flight away from reality, where digital and online worlds constitute a substitution. The question now is how far can the world go before yielding to a permanent state of hyperreality? Perhaps we are already in this state right now; after all, the hyperreal is contagious, like a respiratory virus.

•••••••••••••••••••
i I discussed in-depth the notion of hyperreality in an earlier book Bardo Times (2018)

In my previous book - *Healing the Wounded Mind*[ii] - I discussed the hypothesis that there might be a form of 'mind virus' affecting our human thinking patterns. In this, many people are collectively sensing that something is not quite right with the world but cannot put their finger on it. There is something 'falling apart' around us, as if the backdrop to a theatre play we are watching begins to rip apart, revealing the torn glimpses of another backdrop behind it. The poet W.B Yeats famously wrote, in his poem 'The Second Coming' –

Turning and turning in the widening gyre

The falcon cannot hear the falconer;

Things fall apart; the centre cannot hold;

Mere anarchy is loosed upon the world,

No one can any longer deny the disturbances and unrest that is erupting across the globe, within nations, and within our own communities, and yet we gaze upon them with a sense of the surreal – we are unable to fathom what is truly unfolding around us. The customized bubble of perception-protection is morphing and wobbling, and we struggle to form a sense of meaning from it. Many people are suffering from cognitive dissonance even though they may not know what this phrase means – yet they are experiencing it with increasing frequency (see Chapter Four). Things are no longer adding up, as they say – although this has been the case for a long time. It is as if we have become abstract players within a kind of simulated game – we are being moved across the gameboard as we sit back and passively watch from our armchairs whilst in lockdown.

The world we once knew has shifted into the realm of abstractions. Many of our symbols of connection are now digitally mediated through social media. Our sense of

----
ii   Healing the Wounded Mind: The Psychosis of the Modern World and the Search for the Self (Clairview Books, 2019)

reality is being defragged and reprogrammed through the expanding bubble of the information sphere – the *infosphere*. According to Italian philosopher Franco Berardi,

> The acceleration of info-flows led to the saturation of attention, so that our ability to discriminate between what is true and what is false becomes confused, and disturbed; the storm of info-stimulation blurs the vision, and people come to wrap themselves up in networks of self-confirmation.[1]

Self-confirmation is, on the contrary, now adding to our increasing failure of perception, bringing in a new order of chaos – 'chaos is the measure of the excessive density of the infosphere in relation to the psychosphere.'[2] Chaos spreads and proliferates in the human, biological world - yet order and organization dominates in the world of the machine. Despite the false perception of social stability, civil war is looming as a secular trend in our modern societies. We are moving through a chaotic process across the globe at the same time as a technological order is attempting to assert itself against a rising fragmentation of human chaos, as I discuss in Part Two.

The current cultural relapse is not so much the false information and pseudo-truths but the lack of the social mind to make critical distinction. Part of this is due to the shift from written, textual dominance to the visual interpretation of information.[iii] The world as it currently stands is mutating into an infrastructure run on programmed information and objects - of abstract 'things' – and it is trying to merge with our collective mind. It is acting similar to a field-like mental pathogen, or computer virus:

> ...conscious volition has lost its ability to govern both the flows of social unconsciousness

---

[iii] I discussed this in Ch. 8 of my book The Sacred Revival (2017)

that are spreading chaotically, and the inexorability of the networked automaton.³

There is a sense that a certain rootlessness has crept into the world - a rootlessness of frantic uncertainty mixed with desperate tech-salvation. Things have become more liquid-like as older, established social forms are dissolving faster than new ones can replace them. What we have now is not yet able to form or hold its shape. It feels as if there is a rising confusion entering into the world reality-bubble. Many people are not really sure what's going on 'in' or 'with' the world – and no one is telling us anything.

Social and political systems seem so full of abstract madness partly because they have lost their relation to anything tangible or remotely truthful. Many people are now rushing just to stand still or else being forced to sit still in their homes. The writer Elias Canetti recognized this situation when he wrote - 'A tormenting thought: as of a certain point, history was no longer "real." Without noticing it, all mankind suddenly left reality; everything happening since then was supposedly not true; but we supposedly didn't notice.'ⁱᵛ

We have hardly noticed that we now live surrounded by a melting consensus that has yet to be transformed into a new agreed upon collective consensus. And this in-between state of fluidity is being exploited and manipulated by global players attempting to program a global mindset with a new dominant narrative favourable to their aims (of technologized governance). Older forms of consensus thinking have been fragmenting rapidly ever since the 2020 pandemic was released upon the world. Within only a few months people had their routines, their beliefs and certainties, their social alliances, all fragmented and placed into shock therapy. Such shocks are well-known and well-documented processes to defragment a person's mind before programming

••••••••••••••••••
iv   Taken from his collection of personal writings from 1942 to 1972 called The Human Province.

it with new input. This form of reprogramming has similar traits to that described by Naomi Klein in her book *The Shock Doctrine* - a shock destabilizes a situation (and the psyche) so that within this state of instability and vulnerability, a new narrative (programming) is introduced. That is, the psyche is 'de-branded' so that it can be 're-branded.' From *shock* to *logo* – just do it with a swish and with a *yes, we can*. Without knowing it, our memories are being shuffled so that they can be branded with magical memes and logos direct from the thought-police. It is no fantasy to recognize that human memory is now subject to constant rewriting and rearrangement. Freud was aware of this a century ago: 'the material present in the form of memory traces being subjected from time to time to a *rearrangement* in accordance with fresh circumstances - to a *retranscription*.'[4]

Human perception is caught within its own distortion bubble. Generally, the human mental operating system – often referred to as the 'intellect' - has no access *outside* the system as it makes decisions and understanding based upon information within the system. It can only interpret and select from within the system, and generally follows its dominant logic or narrative. It has no genuine free choice, only the space to select from a limited range. As Adorno and Horkheimer mentioned in their *Dialectic of Enlightenment* – 'False clarity is only another name for myth.'

The myth that is now being thrust upon global civilization is one attempting to cultivate a new dominant narrative – a *global mind change* through fragmenting and re-programming of the human collective consciousness. It is an audacious plan. Impressive maybe, but scandalous all the same. As is well known, each culture seeks to promote and condition those ideas which support and maintain its legitimacy. What each society fears is a flight from their dominant worldview. The 'national imperative' has been the programming of nation states since their inception. If you wanted to belong, you had to agree to the program. Yet what happened was that many different nations went to war over their different programming. And millions upon millions of people lost their lives because of them either agreeing, or being forced, to adhere to their national programming. The world since then has gone global. What is needed now is not a national program but a global one. A global programming can be controlled and managed from the top by a very few people. What was needed, however, was a global 'shock' to bring the world to a halt. This *global halt* has just been applied through the 2020 pandemic, as I explain further in Part Two. And now, the 'new program' is being dutifully supplied.

The mental virus that represents this new dominant narrative will try out all sorts of manipulations and manoeuvrings to construct a social consensus, despite the present fluidities. The contemporary person today exists under a collectivist mentality, and in order not to ask too many questions they are provided with a life of increasing abstraction and distraction. As the philosopher Chantal Delsol says: the modern person 'seeks a predictable, ready-to-wear kind of happiness at a bargain price.'[5] Unfortunately, that kind of social happiness no longer comes at a bargain price. It will come with a price-tag of biosecurity and digital surveillance. Adhering to the new programmed reality will come at a heavy cost to individual freedoms – physically and perceptually.

Thankfully, it is still possible for those with critical faculties to perceive the incoming, and oncoming, collective 'consensus programming' for what it is. The 'Great Reset' agenda is pushing for greater digitization and automation of human life, and this includes control over thinking patterns too.[v] Increasing fragmentation within the machinery of social life brings greater automation. There is a new howl coming after the *Howl* of poet Allen Ginsberg –

• • • • • • • • • • • • • • • • •
v   Schwab, Klaus; Malleret, Thierry - COVID-19: The Great Reset

I saw the best minds of my generation destroyed by madness,

starving hysterical naked,

dragging themselves through the negro streets at dawn

looking for an angry fix,

angelheaded hipsters burning for the ancient heavenly connection

to the starry dynamo in the machinery of night[vi]

The new present 'howl' is also burning 'for the ancient heavenly connection' in the 'machinery of night' – it is howling for *any* connection as things fall apart from the centre. As Elias Canetti said - all of a sudden, we left reality, and everything happening since then is supposedly not true. The symbols of this meltdown are getting stronger all the time. One of the most powerful symbolic forms of modern times is our economic exchange – money. Money is now targeted by the Great Reset for a new life of digital abstraction as a cashless society is close to implementation. When the financial system finally becomes abstracted into the intangible then it shall morph further into automation. The move into a cashless economy and into the expected central bank digital currencies (CBDCs) is a glaring sign of the new consensus reality construction.

The infosphere, the arising tech-security apparatus, and the soon-to-be digitized economy are forming the infrastructure of the new perceptual reality paradigm. They are like the intangible realms poised to subject us to ever more forms of power relations that will become standardized. Italian philosopher Franco Berardi considers power and authority to be now dispersed amongst our social systems to the point that their ubiquity makes resistance almost futile. Soon, he says, it will be like struggling back against

---

vi   Taken from the poem Howl written by Allen Ginsberg (published 1956)

the air. Berardi notes that – 'Not the body but the soul becomes the subject of techno-social domination.'[6]

The virus *we* need to watch out for is the one that infiltrates our thinking and attempts to program human perceptions. It is a virus that attempts to silence and censor free speech and turns debt into a weapon to keep people dependent upon the external system. The incoming narrative-under-construction that is to form the 'new worldview' will use symbolic forms of power – such as health, security, economy – as tools for psychic and social suppression. As the Italian journalist Ezio Mauro puts it:

> 'I am indebted, I am dependent upon images and concepts. I am a customer-citizen: indeed, a consumer. I buy and receive ideas pre-processed and broadcast in forms that are functional to someone else's narrative. I am not required to make any sort of effort in exchange for waiving my right to any form of autonomy…I am unable to give shape to a worldview. Eventually, I will not even have an image of myself in connection with others.'[7]

Are we being manoeuvred into giving away the rights to create our own worldview? If so, then we need to be asking ourselves what can be done before a great many people across the world are forced into accepting a replacement consensus reality that will be highly dangerous to our lives as independent, free-thinking individuals.

Perhaps it is time to acknowledge the global wounding in order to find the correct form of healing. As the indigenous people of Bioko like to say – 'Let us get nearer to the fire, so that we can see what we are saying.'

The thing is, for far too long we've had a dominant 'prophesizing' media directing predictive programming and dystopian memes to us. Maybe we need to get even closer to the fire still.

THREE

Prophesizing Media

(or Predictive Programming?)

*'Now the death of God combined with the perfection of the image
has brought us to a whole new state of expectation.
We are the image'.*

John Ralston Saul, *Voltaire's Bastards*

The information and inputs people receive, and process, affects one's sense of reality. Everything is a question of perception. And the mind (the intellect and the emotions) form the sense of perception that then shapes, naturally, our perceptual reality. The bubble of perception that forms one's reality is not a solid structure. It is fluid and continuingly shifting, readapting, and, from time to time, it wobbles. Recently, this consensus reality bubble that so many, for so long, have attached their senses to, has been fluctuating oddly. We have seen that concepts and notions of what is 'true' and 'false' have lost their footing. The things we believed in - those things, people, or institutions we placed our trust in; those things we relied upon; the sense of a solid future – all this has become fluid and is vulnerable to nudges, tweaks, and manipulations. This has been going on for a number of years now – only that it went into overdrive during the year 2020.

The previous years have seen a large wave coming into formation of dystopian memes that were projected through various media platforms – books, films, and art. This wave of dystopian memes has become a major part of modern, mostly western, popular culture in recent years. We may not have been aware of it, yet the media began to prophesize – or was it an uncanny predictive programming? It appears we may have been self-programming ourselves through the memes all the time. It is as if we are living through times of auto-exploitation where we have given us permission to exploit ourselves. *To prophesize is to meme.*

A meme is a unit of memorization, a unit of significance, embodied in a sign, phrase, or image - or all three. It is a jingle, jangle, catchy catch-all that can be easily replicated, and it clings to the memory cells like an artificial virus: 'The proliferation of memes in the mind-scape of our time is an effect of the transition from the alphabetical to the immersive infosphere.'[1] The info and public sphere has been invaded and colonized by a contagion of memes (and critical thought is hiding in the closet eating a take-out pizza). The disturbances in our collective reality bubble – what I call the consensus reality meltdown - is creating psychological, physical, and emotional impacts that are affecting our overall well-being. The mainstream media participates in and promotes the mutating of the consensus reality narrative through sensationalizing specific, targeted events. They seize upon a particular topic that enflames the collective imagination, and then they fuel this in-line with the dominant agenda. Rather than averting disaster we now indulge in thoughts of survival or disaster preparation, fulfilling the prophecies that have been handed to us. We have come to accept that something's coming and it's going to hurt – whatever it is. In this way, we are dealing with many 'thought-viruses' alongside the biological ones. The many and varied uncertainties are fuelling a rise in dissonance, discomfort, and detachment. We may have been unwittingly engaging in auto-exploitation, unknowingly programming ourselves, as the dystopian memes dance wildly.

Dystopian Memes

It is psychologically known that when an inner psychic or unconscious desire is not consciously realized or processed, then it will seek to be manifested in the external world. The inner urge (or shadow) will seek for its expression through other means – whether cathartic or destructive. As Carl Jung noted, 'The unconscious works sometimes with most amazing cunning, arranging certain fatal situations, fatal experiences, which make people wake up.'[2] Jung was optimistic that such situations can work to trigger people into more conscious awareness - to make people 'wake up' to the situation. This may explain the recent wave of dystopian cultural artefacts that have arrived on our shores.

In terms of non-fiction books in the English-language world, there have been many in the last two decades that have dealt specifically with long-term 'catastrophism' as it is called. These include, but are not limited to, the following: *Our Final Century* (Rees, 2003), *Collapse* (Diamond, 2005), *Catastrophes and Lesser Calamities* (Hallam, 2005), *The Party's Over* (Heinberg, 2005), *The Next World War* (Woodbridge, 2005), *The Upside of Down* (Homer-Dixon, 2006), *The Long Emergency* (Kunstler, 2006), *The Revenge of Gaia* (Lovelock, 2006), *When the Rivers Run Dry* (Pearce, 2006), *The Suicidal Planet* (Hillman, Fawcett, Raja, 2007), *The Shock Doctrine* (Klein, 2007), *Field Notes from a Catastrophe* (Kolbert, 2007), *With Speed and Violence* (Pearce, 2007), *The Next Catastrophe* (Perrow, 2007), *An Uncertain Future* (Abbott, 2008), *Reinventing Collapse* (Orlov, 2008), *World at Risk* (Beck, 2009), *Time's Up!* (Farnish, 2009), *Down to the Wire* (Orr, 2009), *Requiem for a Species* (Hamilton, 2010), *Tropic of Chaos* (Parenti, 2011), *Living in the End Times* (Zizek, 2011), *Convergence of Catastrophes* (Faye, 2012), *The Great Disruption* (Gilding, 2012), *Crisis*

Without End? (Gamble, 2014), *After Fukushima: The Equivalence of Catastrophes* (Nancy, 2014), *The Collapse of Western Civilization* (Oreskes, Conway, 2014), *The Resilience Dividend* (Rodin, 2014), *The Sixth Extinction* (Kolbert, 2015), *In Catastrophic Times: Resisting the Coming Barbarism* (Stengers, 2015), *Crime and the Imaginary of Disaster: Post-Apocalyptic Fictions and the Crisis of Social Order* (Yar, 2015), and many more.

Also, the following are just a selection of popular books and/or films from within the same time frame: *Oryx and Crake* (2003), *The Road* (book, 2006; film, 2009), *Children of Men* (book, 1992; film 2006), *The Age of Stupid* (2009), *The Year of the Flood* (2009), *The Book of Eli* (2010), *The Hunger Games* (book, 2008; film 2012), *MaddAddam* (2013), *Snowpiercer* (2013), *The Giver* (book, 1993; film, 2014), *Automata* (2014), *The Maze Runner* (book, 2009; film, 2014), *Divergent* (book, 2011; film, 2014), *Mad Max – Fury Road* (2015), *Ready Player One* (2018), *The Testaments* (2019).

Recent years have seen a wave of both A and B-movies dealing with post-apocalyptic survival, post-oil and post-water scenarios, ramshackle communities, individualist survival, and the list goes on.

These memes and ideas present the human collective mind with the thesis that continuous improvement and progress is not an automatic given. In fact, societies can very easily collapse and fall into ruin. They show that a regression in human nature is likely after such an event, with people likely to turn cannibalistic *(The Road)*, totalitarian *(The Hunger Games)*, or tribal and barbaric *(Mad Max)*. Many of these catastrophist books and films share a common thread in that social order breaks down in the absence of social control and consensus values – that is, 'collective conditioning.' Further, that stronger, authoritarian regimes are needed to maintain a post-collapse form of strict order.

New forms of order and control are essential to manage limited resources, material goods, and human survival. Suppression and repression are the ever-present themes within dystopian narratives.

The potential for this dystopian meme to be realized is already within our current civilization. It may already be partially unfolding through a cascade of interlinked processes that include biosecurity, civil unrest and instabilities, techno-control, and the push for a global economic 'Reset.' What is also being planted in the now fluid splintered consensus reality is the inevitability of some form of impending disaster and a fatalism concerning the future. Another consequence of the dystopian, or catastrophic, meme is that powerful technologies – usually related to governance and security - may be the only solution for humanity's continued survival. We only have to look at China to see how this theme is unfolding rapidly.

It is interesting in this regard that the award-winning cyber-punk novelist William Gibson once commented that he omitted certain dystopian ideas from his novels as he did not wish to be held responsible for helping to bring them about. Alongside the dystopian meme of social collapse, also worthy of mention are the ever-popular zombie and virus-pathogen memes. In recent years, our entertainment screens have been overridden with the walking dead. Some of these popular zombie-based series include: *The Walking Dead*; *The Last Ship*; *Z Nation*; *Fear the Walking Dead*; *iZombie*; *Santa Clarita Diet*; *Black Summer*; *Daybreak*; *Dead Set*; *Kingdom*; *Reality Z*; and many more too numerous to catalogue. And then there are all the recent films and TV series dealing with virus outbreaks and containments, featuring bands of survivors, etc. Really, there are just too many to mention here. Is this upsurge in pathogen pandemics just a mere entertainment coincidence – or is there an element of predictive programming at play? If anything, all of these themes together make for a very strong 'apocalypse archetype' within the collective mind.

The 'apocalypse-pathogen-virus-zombie-endgame' (APVZE) meme has embedded itself deep within the human psyche and is 'amusing ourselves to death,' as Neil Postman would say.[i] Perhaps modern entertainment culture is simply mirroring our own inherent fear-curiosity over the End Times, as played out in the early stages of the 21st century through the 'Millennium Bug,' then 9/11, and later the '2012 death-of-civilization' scare. Indeed, John's 'Book of Revelation' in the New Testament (often called the Apocalypse of John) has the Beast 666 as not only a mark of celluloid entertainment but now as the much discussed 'mark of the beast' which enters into society through human chipping, barcodes, tagging, and other forms. Dystopian memes may be more than mere performance entertainment – they are possibly part of the predictive programming that blurs the line between the unconscious mind and its external manifestations. As the philosopher Franco Berardi remarked,

> 'Art, poetry, narration, music, and cinema trace a landscape of imminent darkness: social de-evolution, physical decay, and neuro-totalitariansim…The art-scape of the new century seems crowded with dystopian imaginings, depressing descriptions of the present, and frightening scenarios of the imminent time to come.'[3]

The risk here is that dystopian memes may in some way be manifested through our collective dreaming as the 'frightening scenarios of the imminent time to come.' As a more recent example, the film 'Songbird' was quickly filmed within four weeks during the July-August quarantines of 2020, and released on December 11th 2020.[ii] It's premise is a dystopian world of 2024 where the covid-19 virus has mutated and the world is in its fourth 'pandemic year.' The film depicts a United States where people infected with the virus are taken

---

i See Postman, Neil. 1985. Amusing Ourselves to Death: Public Discourse in the Age of Show Business. New York

ii https://en.wikipedia.org/wiki/Songbird_(film)

from their homes against their will and forced into quarantine camps, also known as "Q-Zones" (Concentration Camps) with brutal and harsh conditions. In these camps, the infected are left to die or to recover from their own means. Is this only pure entertainment, one wonders?

The real pandemic could perhaps be coming through the contagion of meme viruses that affect the mind.

A Pandemic of the Mind

The Scottish psychiatrist R.D. Laing pointed out that our species has a strong in-built capacity for self-deception, and that we have literally 'tricked ourselves out of our own minds.' Modern western civilization, though outwardly highly developed and technologically advanced, is inwardly still immature, and psychologically under-developed. We have not fully learned how to take back our minds; that is, to have full control over how our own minds are used. Or, to put it another way, to decondition ourselves against disingenuous programming – those opinions, ideas, and perspectives - that are fostered upon us from external sources.

Today, in an age of global communications and social media, we are witness to how a collective mental programming can easily become a pandemic. Dominant institutions – such as politics, economy, and health, etc. – are carriers in the same way as the media is through TV, books, films, and artwork. Most people don't realize the potential for collective instability to be carefully managed as a 'new normal.' As R.D. Laing famously said, insanity is a perfectly rational adjustment to an insane world. The madness of our world has become so pervasive that it has become normalized. We have become conditioned to the illogical and inhumane way the world works and programmed to accept a mutated reality.

The current disturbances unfolding around the world are what Jung referred to as symptoms of the 'totalitarian psychosis.' They are also timely reminders of the critical role that our mental states play in formation of worldly events. Never before in human history have we had the possibility to manifest the human psyche on a global scale. Jung hit the nail squarely on the head when he stressed that we become enlightened by making the darkness conscious. In other words, he was saying that the very thing that is a destructive force can also be a liberating one. The very thing that puts us to sleep can also wake us up. This may be true. Yet the question we still need to ask is – are we going to be awakened into yet another dream?

We are living through a period of immense psycho-stimulation. The impacts we receive, or which we choose to allow ourselves to be open to, will shape our perceptions during the formation of a new consensus reality. They are likely to affect how we may be a part of the dominant narrative or independent from its influence. We are living in an age of techno-cultural mutation. Many things are shifting, and this is only going to accelerate further. In these fluid times, the prophesizing media is rich in predictive programming that is, to various degrees, creating a disequilibrium in the human psyche. The social body is merging with an increased digitalization and techno-infrastructures that are transforming the very fabric and inducing mutations within this social body. These new flows are fragmenting the collective psychic rhythm – 'The acceleration of media flows stimulating the collective brain is breaking the frame of the rhythm that we inherited from the modern age.'[4] A mutation has arisen, and it is affecting our perception and perceptions upon reality. This mutation must be recognized in order to understand our conscious relation with the world. What can now be seen is a focused attempt at the shaping of social perception in order to foster a consensus projection of the world that at its core is aimed at social discipline. It can be said that humanity is experiencing a time of active and intense enforced socialization.

According to Franco Berardi, we have entered into *technomaya* and we are being forced to undergo a changed set of experiential relations with the world. The predictive programming potentials have 'given the media the power to act directly upon the mind, so that the mediasphere casts a spell that envelops the psychosphere.'[5] Can we resist the mutation?

FOUR

Hyperreality (or Mutation?)

'So long as an illusion is not recognized as an error, it has a value precisely equivalent to reality.'

Jean Baudrillard

With the increasing presence of a merged digital-physical landscape, there is an attempt to create a seamless fuse between these spaces into one conjoined social-cultural-political body that can be seen as the *hyperreal*. This is the space where people become participants in their own psychic ambivalence, contradictions, and uncertainties. There is presently a rapid explosion of the 'hyper' occurring in modern societies that mark their contrary excesses – manic consumption and extreme poverty; extreme sports and athletic drugs; violence, terrorism, and politicized peace; anorexia and obesity; frivolity and addictions; bio-security, health fear and excessive sanitization. The 'hyper' is where extreme contradictions come together as opposing trends. It is only in the hyperreal of consensus meltdown where contradictions are smoothed out into the 'new normal.' Such *new normals* are what I would consider as expressions of the 'modern power-machine' (MPM).

The MPM encourages the expression and manifestation of individual desires that can easily lead to pseudo self-fulfillment and superficial social status. The MPM is nothing other than a digital control society that exploits freedom so that people willingly give away their sovereignty for a selection of choice. As philosopher Byung-Chul Han remarks – 'Big Data is a highly efficient psychopolitical instrument...it facilitates intervention in the psyche and enables influence to take place on a pre-reflexive level.'[1] The result, notes Han, is that 'Digital Big Brother *outsources* operations to inmates.'[2] It is such a world as this, driven and managed by digital data, that Han believes represents the end of the individual who possesses free will. The danger here is that individuals are both indirectly and directly persuaded (coerced?) into acting more like spectators than participants; as consumers rather than citizens: 'Free choice is eliminated to make way for a free selection from among the items on offer.'[3] The dumbing down of human cognition is rendering people as passive onlookers waiting for the next bargain purchase.

The cultures of the modern power-machine revel in the euphoric idealism of self-emancipation ratified with the emptiness of politically correct social identities and ideologies. Psychological harassment is now an assault on modern life. Social media 'celebs' and 'influencers' are destabilizing influences upon the psyche more often than not, as they roll with the consensus narrative, and promote its products, rather than question or offer critical analysis (not that we would expect them to!) The modern power-machine is attempting to fragment, or defrag, the human psychological experience in order to rebuild it into a new, dominant consensus psyche. This is the globalization project – the 'global reset' - that is central to a hyperreal consensus age.

The attempt is now to provide the same, or similar, social-political experiences throughout the world. At the heart of this expanding sphere of homogenization is the attempt to re-brand the human psychosphere – the collective psychological space that defines people's cultural identities. A hyperreal and globalized system of social control cannot be effectively managed if there is too much political diversity, disagreement, and critical thinking within the collective psychosphere. In order to 're-form' this rich psychical diversity into a more congealed psychological mass consensus, first a series of fragmentation is required. This is a process well known to practitioners of mind programming. And it appears that the modern power-machine is now attempting to reprogram the collective human psyche upon a global scale.

The Splintered Self

Populations are being culturally bombarded with such contradictory information that many people are unable to find coherence or to make a whole picture out of the shards. That is, the human mind is finding it increasingly difficult to see the patterns and to connect the dots. Many people have increasingly been experiencing forms of cognitive dissonance. One definition of this state is: '**Cognitive dissonance** refers to a situation involving conflicting attitudes, beliefs or behaviours. This produces a feeling of mental discomfort leading to an alteration in one of the attitudes, beliefs or behaviours to reduce the discomfort and restore balance.'[i]

The result of this is that the mind desperately wishes to reduce the discomfort and restore balance by seeking - or being provided with - a coherent picture, or closure. The danger here is that this 'closure' or 'coherent picture' may be provided by an external source, institution, or body (a structure of orthodox 'authority') and many people will jump onto it as a way of gaining closure, and thus comfort. It is generally a minority of persons who seek to find this coherence and closure within ourselves, through their own resources. With the increasing breakdown of social relations, alliances, and bonds, people's consciousness is being further pushed into compartmentalization where events are seen as

••••••••••••••••••
i   Taken from www.simplypsychology.org

random rather than interrelated and meaningful. This lack of meaningfulness will be compensated for by the rise of external attractions and the offer of security from governmental authorities. Critical thought, perceptive observation, and intuitive knowing will be under the continual onslaught of bullying behaviour modification (see Part Two).

As is now evident in the public realm, self-identity (race, sexuality, etc) is becoming a target of division, further creating doubt, anxiety, and social polarization. Psychologically, people are being pushed to acquiesce, submit, and accept the measures that are being implemented as the 'new normal' for the hyperreal age. And the more that people submit, the greater will be their vulnerability to further submission and disempowerment. Bureaucratic regimes and administrative structures will creep further into people's living, work, and leisure lives until a form of what French philosopher Michel Foucault calls *disciplinary power* will dominate over the human condition. New forms of social discipline and collective obedience are fostering an artificial and engineered state of perception. We are right in the middle of a time of intense 'enforced socialization,' or what Edward Snowden recently referred to as an 'architecture of oppression.' For some, the only response to this overwhelming 'architecture of oppression' will be to find their comfort zones – such as sitting in their chairs at home with their 'surrogates' roaming the digital-physical landscape on their part.[ii] Or, as the 2008 computer-animated sci-fi film *Wall-E* depicted, growing lazy and obese while robots cater to all their needs, while indulging in infantile entertainments. We can only hope this shall never be the case.

Humanity has entered unprecedented times. Such times demand an unprecedented response. By doing nothing, we are

---

ii See the sci-fi film Surrogates (2009) or read the book Kiln People (2002) by David Brin allowing our behaviour to be modified and our self-identities to be splintered. It is within this 'splintered' state of mind that a 'new normal' can be programmed into the collective – and thus, individual – human psyche. Such forms of externally derived mental programming have long been used on the human population – we only need to think of propaganda. That such strategical techniques have been used is clearly an affront upon human mental sovereignty. Yet it seems that the notion of 'sovereignty,' in the eyes of external controlling forces, does not apply to humanity. Sovereignty can be defined as 'the full right and power of a governing body over itself, without any interference from outside sources or bodies.'[iii] A human individual is a governing body that has the 'full right and power' over itself *without any interference from outside sources*. This applies both mentally and physically. Clearly, dominant forms of social conditioning get around this right of sovereignty by a form of willing self-compliance. That is, people agree to their forms of conditioning **because they are not seen as such.** It can be argued that no sovereign right has been breached if people willingly accept and/or agree to the external interventions.

The present modern power-machine is attempting to bring in a new extension of its control – aka., social management – through a direct intervention (read: trespass) upon human bodily sovereignty. The hyperreal age of the 'new normal' is re-defining itself as a landscape more amenable to processing a mechanized form of the human life experience in contrast to the biological experience (see Part Three). The physical body, as an unpredictable site of empowerment, is now antithetical to the future plans of an age of global governance that expects a robot-like compliance from the people. Human bodily sovereignty, it now seems, is a site of contestation. Is this the beginning of a new historical era?

• • • • • • • • • • • • • • • • • •

iii   https://en.wikipedia.org/wiki/Sovereignty

The Hyperreal Becomes Hyperhistorical

Luciano Floridi, a professor of philosophy and the ethics of information, believes that human civilization is shifting into a phase of 'hyperhistory.'[4] A hyperhistorical society that is dependent upon integrative technologies, says Floridi, could also become human-independent – that is, not needing us. Life on this planet is being developed into an infrastructure that favours machinic intelligence and artificial organisms, thus de-territorializing the human experience. Urban environments may soon be more conducive to artificial life than biological ones. No one is yet ready for the mutation at hand. We are being programmed to take on a new position in the world that will erode the possibility of human empowerment - a world where the 'flesh robot' will eventually become the reality consensus.

What is rapidly unfolding across the world is an unprecedented migration of human interaction from its physical space to the digital-sphere. And this also happens to be an environment of increasing surveillance and technocratic social management. The incoming generations will recognize no fundamental difference between the digital-sphere and the physical world as this mergence will form the reality they are born into. To the new generations, the digital-physical-sphere will be their only reality for they will have been born without the offline-online distinction. In the words of Luciano Floridi, they were born *onlife*. This is now their reality, and it is 'onlife.' The world that many of us recognized as being fundamentally human will never be the same again. With the 'onlife' mode, a new era of history begins. Childhood comes to an end when they stop being a child and become a user. It is then that they inhabit whole new realities – realities they may believe to be 'user-generated' when in fact the reverse is more the case.

Connectivity and access will be part of the regime of the new power-machine. And the rights of access are going to be a matter of consensus health That is, to be a part of the 'new consensus reality' will mean opting-in to its sanctioned, and on-surveillance, connections (as I explore further in Part Two). Soon, opting out will be made an almost impossible alternative. Connecting into the power-machine will become the new cartography of the 'human reality.' Living 'manually' will become one of the last few remaining sites of resistance as human life becomes regulated-by-automation.

As stated, the environment in which we live and thrive may soon be more conducive to artificial life than biological ones. This *may* be the natural progression of a technological trajectory within evolving civilizations. It could equally be the result of a global management group wishing to accelerate the process. Are we ready for the mutation at hand?

The infosphere, which is for now where human collective consciousness still interacts, is becoming increasingly populated by algorithms, self-programming software, big data and databases, communication protocols, and the rest. The infosphere is inhabited by entities and agents that are basically *informational* and where interactions are now processed. Living manually is becoming obsolete as life becomes more and more automated. The incoming consensus reality is being programmed to take an 'informational interpretation' of the world. Soon the distinction between online and offline will become increasingly blurred, and eventually will come to the point where there will be little point in asking the question, when we are immersed in our smartphones – in which world am I in? As Floridi says, 'We are witnessing an epochal, unprecedented migration of humanity from its Newtonian, physical space to the infosphere itself as its new environment, not least because the latter is absorbing the former' and the new generations 'will come to recognize no fundamental difference between the infosphere and the physical world, only a change in perspective.'[5]

What people are experiencing more and more around them in such 'modern' societies is a creeping abstraction. We are increasingly feeling distanced as if being moulded into abstract players within a kind of simulated game. A shadow is casting a veil across our eyes, and things are blurring. The once-intangible void is becoming the new reality. We are entering the void.

FIVE

Entering the Void

'The attraction of the void is irresistible.'

Jean Baudrillard

It is increasingly feeling as if the unreal world has taken the place of the real. Are we sure of what is certain, or what's going to matter? The rate of change – of risk – is shooting ahead of our capacity, as a biological organism, to cope. This is part of the current consensus reality meltdown and the unfoldment of a technologically-based reality. Cultural philosophers are now debating, writing, and worrying more and more over ethics because the world is currently changing so fast that traditional systems and understandings are becoming rapidly obsolete. As the world shifts increasingly into a technologized realm, we are entering a void where many people may find it difficult to navigate. The cognitive dissonance that is accompanying this is also indirectly assisting an overarching dominant consensus of security and control to provide the comfort so many people are now seeking.

We are living as if upon the peak of an iceberg whilst below the waterline a whole non-visible and almost intangible world has grown up beyond governance or accountability. A new frontier for old forces has emerged within the great post-2020 reshuffle and is embroiled in a race for powers to colonize and control the digital flows as well as the social sphere. The modern post-pandemic world is shaping up to be a place rife with its own viral-digital epidemics infecting our psyches. The pathogen has found a home within controlled news and censored media. The social body is fragmenting and being subjected to a new rhythm of the modern power-machine. The bottom line is that the world is creating a disequilibrium in the human psyche.

According to the World Health Organization, in the last forty-five years suicide rates have increased by 60% worldwide; and these figures do not include unsuccessful suicide attempts, which are said to be up to twenty times more frequent than actual successful suicides.[i] 97.5 million Americans used, or misused, prescription pain pills in 2015, according to the National Survey of Drug Use and Health. Drug overdose deaths have tripled since 2000, and opioid abuse kills more than a hundred Americans daily. According to a recent report published by the *Journal of the American Medical Association* (JAMA) 16.7 percent of 242 million U.S. adults reported filling one or more prescriptions for psychiatric anti-depressant drugs in 2013.[ii] This is one in every six people and is an increase from 13 percent in 2012. And these are the figures prior to the 2020 pandemic. Anxiety and depression are endemic also amongst celebrity culture. Many well-known celebrities are in therapy, or have been in therapy, or are in dire need of therapy; for ailments ranging from alcohol and drug abuse, failed relationships, stress, and other factors.

Many people are presently suffering from post-traumatic stress disorder, panic attacks, attention deficit disorders, and an undirected rage against the modern power-machine. These are symptoms of a disturbance that is affecting our psychic stability. And in this psychic state, we are stepping forth into the void where a fluid reality awaits.

---

i   See http://www.who.int/mental_health/prevention/suicide/suicideprevent/en/

ii   For more information, see http://jamanetwork.com/journals/jamainternalmedicine/article-abstract/2592697

The Social Simulacrum

The world that is perceived 'out there' is a projection of the inputs we have received; that is, it is the brain's best guess based on the data available. And since most people's brains work in a similar manner, the final projection onto life's movie screen has been, more or less, an agreed consensus. The general state of human perception is based on an internal simulation that the physical apparatus (the body-mind) has interpreted for us. This means that technically life as we know it is a simulation, or simulacrum – *an image or representation of someone or something*. We live in an observer-influenced reality, just that most of the time our observations seem to correspond to what we 'know' as life. Mystical literature through the ages has spoken about our reality as being, in some form or other, an illusion – as not *real*. Of course, life still feels very real to us: we get hurt, endure pain (sometimes horrific, inhumane pain), and we suffer as well as we love and experience joy. Yet we are still told that it is all an illusion in that it is only a copy of a greater truth. As Plato would say, it is a shadow of the original Pure Form. Overall, reality as perceived is a fluid and malleable phenomenon. And right now, what we are experiencing is a change in our understanding of this phenomenon. The world, and our sense of reality, is mutating and humanity hasn't yet fully upgraded its faculties to correctly interpret this. We are losing our sense of *context*. We see the phenomena yet are finding it harder and harder to fully place it in a context of significance. Societies are organisms of communication, information, and meaning. Those organisms are now morphing.

As human beings, sense perceptions are entangled with the social and cultural environment. As these environments shift, change, and mutate, we shall expect changes too in our organs of perception. Yet if our perceptions are manipulated and/or tampered with, then we have a distorted view of the world. It now seems that human communication has shifted from a vertical Tower of Babel to a horizontal one – into a web that excludes almost nothing, stretching out to ever-expanding, pervasive frontiers. Reality has always been a realm of signs that humans had to learn how to navigate and interpret. As we further engage in this ubiquitous space of signs and influences, authoritative powers are rushing to solidify their own position.

    A crisis has come upon us, seemingly out of nowhere. The growing crisis is not only one of the flesh – our physical health, jobs, family and social institutions – but also of the human mind. It renders our psyche disenfranchised, fragmented, and in disarray, as if loose from its moorings. There is political skepticism and apathy, and great amounts of seething resentment against incumbent political systems all over the world. A good deal of thinking people have come to realize that the forms of democracy presented to us are a sham, and that political systems are rigged from the inside out. Money, power, unseen cabals, global elites, criminal networks, offshoring practices, and illicit deals are what make much of the world turn. Individual voting is nothing more than mass appeasement. There are grand systems within systems that constrain, control, and keep most people in check during their day to day lives. Yet amidst this crisis, the visibility of this inequity has never before been so evident.

    Governments, in the western world especially, are façades for a monopoly of power that operates from behind with an almost unseen hand. The full-frontal farce of politics, on the other hand, is propped up by flashy marketing and slick speeches. The real power lies beyond the nation state and moves between the spaces that constrain the rest of us. It is a power that attempts to increasingly restrict free movement within its spaces by monopolizing the information over anything that moves. And now, as I explain in Part Two, this power is redesigning itself as a new form of biopower.

Individuals, groups, and communities across the world are becoming embroiled and immersed in a global web of false ideologies and power that most people are not aware of. It is almost imperceptible behind the hand of the state and its institutions. Forms of power pervade the physical and digital spaces that are increasingly closing the perimeters. Who can resist or pull back from a fluid web of power that does not seemingly promote itself and yet is promoted by others? It has no name, no theory, no banners or webpages. And yet everyone supports it by not unsupporting it. It becomes a part of us by *giving us its dominant narrative*. It even provides the anomalies too.

The Anomalies within the Consensus Narrative

The consensus narratives now being readjusted into place will attempt to become established by also allowing their own anomalies. A reflection of this can be seen at the end of the second Matrix film (*Matrix Reloaded*) where the Architect (a Freud lookalike) says that the Matrix was reprogrammed to incorporate all of its anomalies into the new program. That is, even anomalies are needed to keep the program running for they are a part of the program itself. It is a totally inclusive reality-set that has no exterior.

In a similar manner, many social systems promote, even unashamedly, those aspects which may appear as the anomalies. Music artists who rage against society - such as singers whose pop-rock songs protest the system - are all massively promoted by the very same system that gets rich from them. Such anomalies are not only tolerated or accepted - they are also actively encouraged. The system, or reality program, seeks to incorporate all genuine alternatives. Everything feeds into the same perception-set. The world that we think we know is being represented to us through a series of overlapping stories, or narratives, that create the impressions of a consensus. Life is then lived and experienced through this medium of an agreed reality perspective.

We rarely stop to consider that *we* have made all this real through our own stories – through those narratives fed to us by society. Our reality consensus is a collection of stories built upon stories.

Whether we wear a turban, sport a long beard, shave our heads, or dress in particular types of clothing, we are indicating to those whom we meet that we adhere to a particular narrative. When people are willing to die to go to paradise; to kill to bring glory and honour; or to destroy lives for a few bank digits – they are all adhering to their stories. And stories only have value if there is a common consensus. It is the same with money, whether it is fiat currency or hard metals, as they have a certain value because there is a consensus story around them. Yet what good is a bar of gold if you are dying of thirst in some desert and the only camel driver with water does not accept your gold? A consensus agreement brings cultural value.

It is the social stories that form structures of meaning which have validity within a corresponding network of stories. Once we encounter another social structure of stories that do not tally with ours then we usually end up going to war with them. Each story we tell ourselves is mutually reinforced within our own network, confirming its validity, until we end up believing what everyone else around us believes. Each particular reality-set uses language, images, social rituals and cultural reinforcements, specifically to create completely aligned reality perceptions. By understanding these stories, or narratives, we are best placed to decode the cultural programming. Humanity literally lives within a world of fiction. And in a world of fictions and stories, the 'greater reality' will always lose out. The 'bigger picture' has always been forced to fit our stories of the world – and always will. Whether we are told the world is flat; that the earth is the center of the solar system; or that we will go to hell if we are bad. The consensus of storytelling will always force a greater reality out of the picture. We live within a sea of stories, and these are the programmed realities that rally for our agreement. What is occurring now, I contend, is a push for people to accept certain dominant narratives on a global scale. This is part of the 'hijacking of reality' that persists in this time. As Albert Einstein once said: 'Reality is merely an illusion, albeit a very persistent one.'

What humanity is largely experiencing today is the moral uncertainty that precedes a new consensus reality as the old narratives begin to fragment. As long as the majority of people expect all problems to be solved outside of themselves then our societies will continue to be dominated by those unruly forces we seldom recognize. The question of human freedom from these forces depends upon people willing to assume the responsibility of critical analysis, acute observation, and awareness. The power for change begins and ends with the individual and should not be from the hands of a minority elite. The question of human responsibility is to resist the forces of dehumanization. If we do not become aware of how our perceptions are managed and influenced by the coercion of external narratives, then we are vulnerable to the encroaching forces of social-technological control, as I shall explore in Part Two.

PART TWO

The Resetting of New Narratives

SIX

Defragmenting the Mind

'Humankind cannot bear very much reality.'

T. S. Eliot

People around the world are now beginning to gradually climb out of their quarantined cocoons of shock and are seeing a new and different world in its place. The result of the 'covid consciousness' that has infected us globally can have the effect of triggering people into stimulated, new perceptions about the nature of their world reality – or it can force them into accepting a 'new normal' consensus reality for the foreseeable future. Are we to come out of our 2020 cocoons with a butterfly consciousness, or do we retain the caterpillar's mind?

This is not a narrative about viruses, or dead infectious parasites – this is a tale of contagious sentient life. From my perspective, what I see is that human life has been radically halted – the brakes applied – as if being placed under a microscope for our own viewing. We have been compelled to view and *to see* ourselves in a way that has never been done before. Humanity has been placed into its largest experiment, and we are the test cases. Across the globe, diverse societies and cultures have been forced into an unprecedented 'stop' as our everyday lives were pressed to a halt. This forced stoppage reminds me of a physical-psychological exercise used by the Greek-Armenian mystic G.I.

Gurdjieff. He named this as his 'stop' exercise. According to Gurdjieff:

> ...at the command "stop," or at a previously arranged signal, every student must instantly stop all movement, wherever he may be and whatever he may be doing...while he is in this state of arrested movement, the student must also arrest the flow of his thoughts, not admitting any new thoughts whatever...this is simply a movement interrupted at the moment of passage from one posture to another... generally we pass from one posture to another so rapidly that we do not notice the attitudes we take in passing. The "stop" exercise gives us the possibility of seeing and feeling our own body in postures and attitudes which are entirely unaccustomed and unnatural to it... the style of the movements and postures of every epoch, every race and every class is indissolubly connected with distinctive forms of thought and of feeling. And they are so closely bound together that a man can change neither the form of his thought nor the form of his feeling without having changed his repertory of postures...[i]

This extract illustrates that its function was to give the 'student' a necessary moment for unhindered self-observation. A person, remarked Gurdjieff, is generally not aware as they pass from one posture to another – we are 'entirely unaccustomed' to this point of observation to the extent that it is unnatural to us. The only way to enforce this is through an externally produced *state of arrested movement*. Gurdjieff also states that every epoch, race, and class have their distinctive forms of thought which are so tightly bound to their 'posture' that they cannot be changed. Later in this description it is remarked that,

---

i   Taken from 'Talks with Gurdjieff' – various online sources

> psychological analysis and the study of the psychomotor functions, applied in a certain manner, demonstrate that each of our movements, voluntary or involuntary, is an unconscious transition from one automatically fixed posture to another, equally automatic...[ii]

If this is considered at the larger scale, it implies that people are culturally bound to particular 'postures' of thought (aka, social conditioning); and that these thoughts and feelings are automatic (programmed). Gurdjieff's method of breaking down these automatisms so that they could be observed was through imposing an external command of 'stop' that had to be obeyed. Likewise, has not the world just experienced a 'stop' exercise enforced upon it by an 'external command' in response to the 2020 pandemic?

For the first time in known history, human civilization in most of its forms was forced to a social, cultural, and – importantly – an economic halt. Global life was stopped in mid-posture – a *state of arrested movement* - and we had to experience a space we are totally unaccustomed to. Furthermore, people are being told that there is no alternative other than a worldwide social-technological-economic 'Great Reset' button to be pressed into play.[iii] On the other side to this we may consider the global 'stop' injunction as an act of 'force majeure,'[iv] whereby humanity is now free from its prior commitments to a way of life it had contracted itself into. The past contract that humanity got itself involved in has now come to represent dysfunctional systems, damaging ideals and beliefs, and a ruinous path to a destructive future. If there was ever a time to break with this contract and to agree upon a new manner of collaboration in going forward, then this *force majeure* offers a unique opportunity.

....
ii   Ibid
iii   See the World Economic Forum's publication: Schwab, Klaus; Malleret, Thierry - COVID-19: The Great Reset
iv   https://en.wikipedia.org/wiki/Force_majeure

Never before has a 'stop' moment like this been simultaneously experienced upon an individual, community, and global level - nor has it previously been possible. For most of humanity's evolution, we – as individuals - existed as localized aspects of psyche and consciousness. We participated in the 'mental life' of those around us and in the community; and later, the country. Only within a relatively short span of historical time has the human species gained a widespread global perspective. Whilst a collective unconscious species mind existed, this lay beneath the conscious awareness of most people. This has now 'flipped over' in that so many more people are currently aware of psychical fluctuations across the world. And I suggest that we are presently experiencing these fluctuations more intensely since the sudden eruption of the 2020 pandemic. This was not possible before, even at the time of the Spanish Flu of 1918-20. Why does this matter? It matters because the effects of consciousness, although seemingly intangible, are just as important as those tangible, physical effects we are generally more aware of.

Consciousness is just as contagious as any biological virus. Perhaps more so, as it is not bound by physical parameters of movement. Consciousness is an open arena – and it spreads like ripples across fluid and intangible, interconnected fields. Each person too creates these ripples, which are then strengthened by larger community and national consciousness fields. Similar to what Gurdjieff spoke of, people create *thought postures* that belong to collectives of human thought. As many readers are aware, like things attract and resonate with like things. It is the same with thought. This is the reason why so many 'like-minded' people group together. They share a common bond in their thinking. At the same time, these physical groupings create collective fields of consciousness. These fields can become powerful and very influential. They have operated throughout extreme cases, such as warfare, where people have behaved against their 'better judgement.' Equally, they have operated during moments of mob violence and mob psychosis. Such collectives of thought are easy to be caught up within – that's why they are contagious. And now, as humanity's collective psyche is growing and developing, such 'contagions of consciousness' are extremely powerful.

Generally speaking, as a person becomes 'socially programmed' by layers of conditioning, they are absorbed into the 'national psyche' of their respective country. This has always operated as a useful function of social management. As a person learns to de-condition themselves, and to throw off these layers of their psychological conditioning, they create more expansive states of awareness by having access to a broader range of consciousness fields. We are each of us affected by the 'consciousness ripples' emanating from others. It is how the ecology of consciousness operates. And since it is an interconnected ecology, individual expansion of awareness does not just remain at the individual level. What each person contributes to their localized fields of consciousness will then go on to form part of a larger body, or consciousness field. And this, ultimately, will form part of a grander resonating field of collective consciousness – at the community, national, and global level. Therefore, *what* and *how* we each think is an important aspect since it adds to a global psyche.

What the world is experiencing now is not only a biological pandemic but also a psychological one. How we feed into this, and *what* is fed into this, will establish the tone of an overall psychic resonance. And this larger field of resonance can be coherent or dissonant, and many other degrees in-between. That is, if a psychological environment of fear, panic, and anxiety is created through thousands, or even millions, of individualized fields of consciousness, these will ripple out to congeal into a grander collective field of increased psychic density. The resonance of disturbance will be on a scale far exceeding the individual level. Similarly, if localized ripples of coherence, hope, trust, and empowerment are transmitted, these will influence both the local and global psychological states. This is not voodoo or magical thinking – it reflects how the intangible energetic realm operates. Psychologically, we are not alone. Each person lives as a part of the world, and not apart from it. In this respect, each individual has a responsibility to manage their thoughts – what they receive and process as well as what they transmit.

Throughout the global 'stop' phase, people's automated movements and automatic thinking patterns were put on hold – into a state of *arrested movement*. It may never happen again. It is likely we shall receive external impacts in our lives that momentarily make us pause as individuals – yet global ones are a very, very rare occurrence. It has been an exceptional moment, and the impacts need to be considered carefully. Many questions have arisen that need to be examined. One of these is the question of brainwashing upon a global level. For example, was the 2020 pandemic used as a strategy for managing a controlled consensus reality? Another thing needed here is perspective. For many, the biological virus and the ensuing pandemic are all part of the same mix. I would disagree. They are not the same – and here's why. One of these elements (the virus) is a biological entity that exists principally within organic bodies and is governed by the laws of nature. The other element (the pandemic) is a social-cultural-political response governed by human-made laws. One is natural; the other is not. And what concerns me, as I explore further in these writings, is not so much the behaviour of the biological virus but rather the human-made reactions and related power-relations. As they say, judge a person by the company they keep. And I am 'judging' – or critically questioning – the virus by the artificial company of the politically-motivated pandemic response. The virus and the pandemic are not the same thing - any more than a car and its driver is the same thing. One is a biological entity, and the other is an artificial (i.e., non-organic) construct that has been established as a vehicle to encapsulate and propel it. Or, to frame it differently – one is an event, and the other is a narrative or myth.

The process of social engineering is a form of 'mythological engineering,' according to researcher and scientist Jacques Vallee:

> Mythological engineering - the deliberate creation of social movements to serve either as opportunity for experiment, as outlets for personal fantasy, or as a vehicle for more down-to-earth political purposes.[1]

The deliberate creation of 'mythological events' is a way of affecting both the conscious and the unconscious mind, which then can create a rift in the human psyche and a 'splintered' perception of reality. Such a rift leads inevitably to a form of irrationality that then can adjust itself through 'mythological engineering' into a range of social-cultural 'new norms.' Such irrational psychology, I argue, is more prevalent than most people realize. Again, it forms a part of the engineering of 'myths to believe in.' Again, as Vallee states – 'Human actions are based on imagination, belief, and faith, not on objective observation...And to control human imagination is to shape mankind's collective destiny.'[2] I would agree with Vallee's observations that myths, in various forms, are often utilized to serve long-term social manipulation purposes. Vallee was observant in his recognition that the key to understanding any type of phenomenon lies in the psychic effects that is produced in the observers. Also, that symbols are more powerful than utterings of the intellect. Again, quoting from Vallee:

> What I do mean is that mythology rules at a level of our social reality over which normal political and intellectual trends have no real power...They are operated upon by symbols, and the language these symbols form constitutes a complete system. This system is meta-logical, but not metaphysical.[3]

Within the transition from an older reality construct into a new consensus reality, symbols hold greater sway over the unconscious mind than do pronouncements. In this context, we may recognize the symbolic power of biohazards and weak bodies (as I shall explore in further depth). Human consciousness is not free from external attempts to impose a control system. And since human life is steered by imagination and myth, then it makes sense that any such control system would seek to condition our belief structures. It would be fair to say that humanity is constantly being tested, sometimes to our limits, to accept previously unimagined ideas. New beliefs and mythologies are being planted into mass human consciousness on a regular basis. The most common response to this is to fit the new data into pre-existing parameters of thought - our 'reality boxes' - in an attempt to stave off the invasion of the irrational. For when the irrational encroaches upon our consensus reality, we often 'close up' or react negatively if we are not able to assimilate it.

There is even more reason then for the human community to come together with at least a minimum of psychological insight. When communities and individuals lack psychological insight, they are open and vulnerable to impulses that impact and influence the unconscious. Unawareness of such forces can bring about emotional, mental, and physical instability. It is a psychological trait that when our minds recognize a repressed force within ourselves, a corresponding expression manifests in the outer, physical world. The images we have within us can be just as powerful as those without. That is why mythology, the imagination, and symbols all hold great sway over us. In the gnostic Gospel of Thomas, it is written that Jesus pronounced: 'If you bring forth what is within you, what you bring forth will save you. If you do not bring forth what is within you, what you do not bring forth will destroy you.' What we repress within our deep unconscious may eventually come to bite us back.

What is being discussed here is nothing less than the re-programming of human life. As I have pointed out, an unprecedented global experiment has just occurred, and is ongoing, with the aim of 're-setting' the consensus reality. As such, the site of engagement is with the concept of the 'healthy self.'

The *healthy self* is one of most central creations of the modern age. The psychology of the 'balanced' human being with its correct internalization and assimilation of social norms, habits and values has been a crucial narrative. The stability of nations has been based on this narrative. Alongside it has been the ongoing discourse about an individual's, and a community's, state of physical and mental health. Such a discourse incorporates the ever-morphing practices of self-responsibility and 'techniques of self' that often play out to self-regulate the population. Through this, many people accept the responsibility to enact their own forms of perpetual auto-surveillance. These practices are, in a way, the expression of contemporary systems to govern the self as a technique of social management. And the latest expression of the *healthy self* is being targeted by the rise of a new form of biopower, as I explain in the next chapters.

SEVEN

The New Reign of Biopower[i]

*'There are forms of oppression and domination
which become invisible - the new normal.'*

Michel Foucault

What people fear most is death and dying. It has been humanity's curse since birth. The modern world, with its increased efficiency and science, debates death more than life. The awareness of suffering and the desire to overcome it are predominant in the modern age. The 'healthy body' and *healthy self* is about the avoidance of suffering and the overcoming of illness, at almost any cost. And, as I remarked at the end of the previous chapter, it is also a target of power. In terms of well-being, it is not just bodies that are exposed, but also the psyche. The distinction between the private and the public body (including the psyche) is specifically a human social-political construct. And what was needed was an 'event' in order to breach that private-public distinction.

The authors of the World Economic Forum's (WEF) *The Great Reset* have stated that these 'Covid times' are 'our defining moment' and that 'we will be dealing with

---

i   An earlier version of this chapter first appeared in the magazine 'New Dawn' (no.183 – Nov-Dec 2020)

its fallout for years, and many things will change forever.'[ii] In the pages of their publication *The Great Reset* the authors brazenly declare of the coming 'economic disruption of monumental proportions, creating a dangerous and volatile period on multiple fronts – politically, socially, geopolitically – raising deep concerns about the environment and also extending the reach of technology into our lives.' We are told that life for many of us is 'unravelling at alarming speed.' Yet what, we may wonder, will be constructed to 're-frame' where this unravelling has taken hold? As the 'new norms' are being unveiled in many societies across the world we are witnessing an attempt to reconstruct and modify a 'new consensus' around everyday reality. Yet this is not all - I suggest that we shall see newly defined, and pervasively employed, forms of biopower in the age of this 'Great Reset.'

A reconfiguration of social-political power has been in process for some time and is now rapidly emerging as part of a medical-political-economic institutional complex that I refer to as the *new reign of biopower*. What was required for this redefinition in the monopoly of power was a 'trigger' that would allow a radical alteration in the legal narratives of claiming control over the categorizations of life and death. With the post-2020 pandemic landscape across the globe now being formed, a post-sovereign world is emerging where biopolitics is giving legitimacy to a network of socializing regimes from biocapitalism to biosecurity. The 2020 lockdowns and quarantine travel measures were only a foretaste of what is to come once the new regimes of biopower become fully institutionalized. Biopower is the new reign attempting to gain dominion over a whole new domain of personal sovereignty.

The French philosopher and social theorist Michel Foucault is well-known for bringing forth the debate on biopower and biopolitics in his work in the mid-to-late

---

[ii] Schwab, Klaus; Malleret, Thierry - COVID-19: The Great Reset

1970s. Initially, Foucault framed his argument in the form of 'disciplinary societies' which he defined as an array of 'corrective institutions' spread across the social field - asylums, factories, schools, hospitals, universities, etc — with each serving to inculcate and condition a mode of conduct and consciousness.[iii] These institutions he placed within the eighteenth, nineteenth, and early twentieth centuries. Above these socializing institutions traditionally stood the sovereign, which later became the State that exercised sovereign power. One of the 'privileges' of early sovereign power was the right to decide life and death - the right of a ruler to seize things, bodies, and ultimately the life of subjects. It was the model of power that was codified in classical politics, and one that has remained essentially unaltered during the transition from sovereign to State. The early birth of biopower in modernity marked the point when the biological life of individuals became the 'political subject' that belonged to State rule. Foucault's description of disciplinary societies was based around power exercised within institutions; in terms of early biopower this was seen as shaping disciplinary health measures as pertaining to the hospital and the asylum particularly. More recently, institutional power has seeped out from the spaces of enclosure into what is now a pervasive, fluid, almost free-floating, administration of power that represents the control societies of the post-sovereign era. We are entering into a world where continuous control will reshape the new era of biopower.

A Post-Sovereign Era: Biopower & Biopolitics

Once biological life is recognized within the framework of the modern state, then it can be included within its governance of power, which then gets interpreted as biopower. And to declare biopower as a form of governance, the State must seek to transform its citizens into *docile bodies* (the 'masses'). Many globalist-influenced forms of State gover-

---

[iii]   See Discipline and Punish by Michel Foucault

nance are directing their newfound biopower against both the individual body and the 'mass body' as a biopolitical target. The modern human condition is such that the individual is not the object but rather the subject of biopower. In many territories, but not all, the State is representing itself as a new style of biopower-driven authority.

i) Biopower

Within the context of a biological threat, the subsequent 'pandemic' was utilized as a social-political construct to re-constitute the 'normalizing' of human society. This so-called, and overly hyped, 'normalizing' of society is enacted by a series of 'power seizures' which has given authority to a newly conceived biopower that claims jurisdiction over the individual and the collective body. This biopower has given itself the 'right' to decide over how to administer life or even death. In short, biopower is concerned with exercising control over the administration of complete life.

In terms of the individual, this enactment of biopower over the human body gives the State the legality to put individual bodies under surveillance and, if need be, punished by incarceration, using biosecurity jurisdiction. This has been exercised in numerous cases recently, as in the 28-year-old Perth woman who broke the Western Australian quarantine rules and was handed a 6-month prison sentence.[iv] The form of biopower that is being exercised under the pandemic 'state of emergency' is concerned with a new mapping of life – social, political, and economic. The management of human existence is undergoing profound redefinition and transition.

Part of this redefinition designates a new narrative that is currently being used to underpin State responses to the Covid-19 pandemic. It is utilizing a language of 'health

iv　　See - https://www.abc.net.au/news/2020-08-25/woman-who-snuck-into-wa-on-truck-handed-six-month-jail-sentence/12592832

risks' for intervention and intrusion into our private lives. This includes the jurisdiction to enter into a person's house without permission to forcibly remove people either considered a health risk or insufficiently 'obeying' quarantine measures. The former was stated by the World Health Organization (WHO) on March 30th 2020 when Dr Michael Ryan (Executive Director of WHO's Health Emergencies Program) gave a statement saying that authorities may have to enter people's homes to remove suspected family members to an 'isolated designated facility.' These measures have now been enacted into law. For example, under the New Zealand state of emergency, police officers now have the power to enter homes to enforce self-isolation rules.[v] In an ironic twist, those citizens opposing such draconian measures are being negatively labelled as 'sovereign citizens' where originally the term sovereign individual meant the moral or natural right of a person to have bodily integrity and be the exclusive controller of their own body and life. Here we see a deliberate twisting of language to now support and enforce the regimes of biopower and the new biopower laws being put into effect across the world. Legality is not the first cause required to create new laws – the *power to create laws* is the first cause.

The new reign of biopower refers to a range of strategies backed by 'specialized medical knowledge' and adopted by the State along with a supporting network of institutions, agencies, and non-state actors. The disturbing trend here is that the State is empowering private military actors as well as 'service officers' and giving them power as authorized officers to enforce the new public health directions.[vi] All such 'authorized officers' are given comparative police state powers to enforce State directives – such as searching

---

[v] See - https://www.stuff.co.nz/national/health/coronavirus/120577868/coronavirus-police-can-now-enter-homes-to-look-for-people-gathering

[vi] https://www.theguardian.com/australia-news/2020/sep/21/overreach-and-overzealous-concerns-over-victorias-proposed-new-police-powers

homes and cars without a warrant - although there is no guarantee that they will be held fully accountable. This has already led to many reports of overreach and overzealous policing. Continuous localized lockdowns, track-and-trace surveillance methods, drone surveillance, the loss of right to protest, and other such measures, are now becoming established as the 'new normal' regimes of biopower as exercised within individual States and nation territories. These forms of control and regulation are without precedent and serve to increasingly affect the psychological well-being of sovereign citizens.

Biopower is now arising as an insidious and dangerous form of global power-relations. It is a form of control that seeks to regulate social life not only from without, such as in mask-wearing and social distancing, but also from within – that is, the collective mass psyche of the population. The concept of biopower seeks to gain dominion over the vital aspects of human existence. Within the field of biopower, the term 'biopolitics' refers to the specific sector that is responsible for creating the strategic policies and practices of intervention into individual, public, and collective life.

ii) Biopolitics

Earlier biopolitical strategies concerned the administration and management of illness and health. Now a newly reconfigured field for biopolitics has been created that binds the individual and the collective into a strengthening mix of the technological, the political, the legal, and the financial. Current biopolitics is clearly tied into the global 'Great Reset' of the restructuring of power and the new regimes that have been rendered into existence by the recent states of pandemic emergency.

Biological life is now at the center of state power – and this will dictate all future agendas. All forms of biopolitical authority are now acting as agents of the State, whether they are governmental or non-governmental bodies, which aligns with a twenty-first century medical totalitarianism. Biopower and biopolitics, along with biocapitalism and biosecurity, are combining to create a totalized and singular form of power. In terms of collective humanity, this involves the biopoliticizing of the human race in order to develop new forms of social management which have as their goal making populations live in 'productive ways' as well as insuring against random and/or planned revolt. In other words, the globalist biopolitical agenda is the formation of control societies and the rendering of human life as 'docile bodies' that have no resistance against State intervention.

The biopolitical agenda also incorporates non-state bodies to enact their strategies – most notably philanthropic organizations, social pressure groups, NGOs, and assorted globalist organizations. The biopolitical field has been extended from annual health check-ups, health insurance, and preventive medicine to now incorporate the Covid-19 pandemic measures of random testing, forced isolation, and updated vaccinations. All human life has now been 'biopoliticized' in the attempt to eradicate not our health risks but all the neutral zones of life. There is almost no refuge from the reach of biopolitics when both the exterior and interior life fall under the jurisdiction of total State control. A person's body, health, and happiness - even a person's right to their 'individual sovereign self' - is now regarded as within the realm of authoritarian biopower. Biopower and biopolitics is a dangerous mix of narratives based upon a monopoly of so-called 'scientific knowledge.'

Furthermore, biopolitics cannot be dissociated from the distasteful subject of eugenics. Eugenics has been shown to have links to groups/institutions, as well as the state, in using medical intervention for the subterfuge of curtailing life. In these current times, biopolitical strategies are clearly linked to a new form of high-tech biocapitalism.

The New Biocapitalism

Non-state bodies have played a key role in the biopolitical agenda, especially since the rise of the private pharmaceutical industry, global healthcare strategies, and tech giants. The emergence of the Human Genome Project (HGP) in the 1990s also contributed to state and non-state intervention into the knowledge-based management of biological life. The new genetic technologies that have come out of the HGP have the potential to add to the arsenal of biopower to create, impose, and induce particular behaviours onto individual and collective bodies through surveillance regimes of genetic screening, testing, and research. These new avenues of bioscience have developed into ever increasing industries to the point where we can now frame the large-scale capitalization of bioscience as the revenue of biocapitalism.

The field of biocapitalism aims to develop and maximize targets for pharmaceutical markets and other healthcare interventions. The administration of biocapital policies upon a great number of the world's population is now technologically possible in a way that was not available before. Not only is it technologically feasible, with the Covid-19 pandemic there is now also a reason for its implementation. There is now credible concern in terms of the crossover where biopolitics plays out in relation to biocapitalism. This is the merger where health (and health economics) combines with the data of surveillance capitalism.

Professor Shoshana Zuboff, the author of the widely acclaimed *The Age of Surveillance Capitalism*, has said that digital connection is now a means to others' commercial ends. With the rapid rise of data collection for commercial gain, Zuboff says that: 'The result is that both the world and our lives are pervasively rendered as information.'[vii] People are reduced to being less than products because they are rendered into being a mere 'input' for the creation of the real product which is the data. Predictions about peoples' futures are sold to the highest bidder so that these futures can be profited from or altered to favour better commercial gains. Zuboff considers surveillance capitalism to be, at its core, parasitic and self-referential – a parasite that feeds on every aspect of every human's experience.

Human experience is considered free to be taken as raw material and it is this that becomes the product of value. From this material, organizations decide to intervene in our lives to shape and modify human behaviour in order to favour the outcomes that are most desirable for commercial gains. Behavioural modification is now in the hands of private capital - and undertaken with the minimal amount of external oversight. At its most basic, humans have been reduced to 'batteries' that produce datasets for algorithms and machine learning to process. What is most worrying is that, by and large, the general populations are uneducated into how their data – especially health data – is being utilized by large corporations to fund their continued dominance over the market. Biocapitalism has been quick to align itself with this accelerating expansion of datasets, data tracing and tracking.

The contact-tracing applications developed by the likes of Google and Apple are likely to gather a huge amount of new data that will only add to their escalating data supply chains. Healthcare and biomedical data collection is doubling every 12-14 months; back in 2012 a Ponemon Institute study found that 30% of all the digital data storage in the world was occupied by the healthcare industry.[viii] It

---

vii https://theintercept.com/2019/03/01/surveillance-capitalism-book-shoshana-zuboff-naomi-klein/
viii https://www.forbes.com/sites/stewartsouthey/2019/06/30/medical-wearables-surveillance-capitalism-and-global-health/

can only be imagined how much that figure has increased in the intervening years. The move to digital has been rapid over the past decade – for example, Electronic Healthcare Records (EHR) adoption rates for U.S. hospitals have gone from 10 to 90 % in that time.[ix] The range of medical wearables on the market are now extensive - and growing. It is no accident that Google set its sights on acquiring Fitbit, the company that creates wearable health devices for tracking peoples' activity, exercise, food, weight, and sleep patterns.

It is now possible to monitor most aspects of an individual's health. It is estimated that remote patient monitoring and health trackers will generate $20 billion annually by 2023.[x] Analysis of digital healthcare data and its use for predictive analytics is profoundly changing the way patients are managed as health wearables becomes part of patients' treatment plans. Patient health data will, without doubt, influence the business models of the biocapital market. And this data will only increase from the 'track & trace' apps most governments are desperately pushing upon their populations. Biocapitalism is firmly embedded within the portfolio expansion of the tech giants. Even a cursory glance at the list of projects owned or invested in by the FAMGA (Facebook, Amazon, Microsoft, Google and Apple) tech giants will show an unsettling array of healthcare projects. Such projects involve medical patient databases, hospital research data, pharmacy retail collaborations, AI research facilities, and insurance. In the autumn of 2018, Google's parent company Alphabet invested $375 million in Oscar Health, a 'next-generation' health insurance company.[xi] According to their CEO, Oscar Health aims to manage people's health care from a reinvented and rebuilt

• • • • • • • • • • • • • • • • • •

ix   ibid
x   ibid
xi   Oscar Health was founded in 2012 by Joshua Kushner, who happens to be the brother of Jared Kushner, President Trump's son-in-law.

technological perspective.[xii]

To say that biocapitalism is divorced from biopolitics would be greatly naïve. In the UK, the government's Secretary of State for Health and Social Care, Matt Hancock, signed an agreement in March 2020 that provides legal backing for the National Health Service (NHS) to set aside its duty of confidentiality in data-sharing arrangements. Named as the 'Covid-19 Purpose,' the new data-sharing agreement means NHS organizations and general medical practitioners (GPs) can share all patient data with any organization they choose, as long as it's for the purpose of 'fighting the coronavirus outbreak.'[xiii]

Alongside the tech giants, the pharmaceutical industry is clearly at the forefront of biocapitalism. Big Pharma is going to make huge profits from the current pandemic situation. And the topic that is currently highest on their agenda is that of vaccinations. The response from many Big Pharma CEOs is that they are calling on society to help finance their research investments. Pharma chief executives have warned governments that they will need to provide substantial upfront funding if vaccines and testing are to be rolled out faster.[xiv] Most Big Pharma Covid-19 vaccine manufacturing costs are expected to be offset by government funding. And the potential outreach is staggering. In a recent report (published August 2020)[xv], public 'health expert' Tony Fauci and epidemiologist David Morens stated that humanity has 'entered a pandemic era.' Their report states that the current pandemic is only the first of many more to come and that we are likely to see an accelerat-

---

xii https://money.cnn.com/2018/08/14/technology/google-oscar-health-insurance/index.html

xiii https://www.computerweekly.com/feature/Surveillance-capitalism-in-the-age-of-Covid-19

xiv https://www.ft.com/content/000a129e-780e-11ea-bd25-7fd923850377

xv https://www.cell.com/cell/fulltext/S0092-8674(20)31012-6#%20

ing rate of future outbreaks in the years ahead.[xvi] What this means is that the future of vaccine rollouts is secured, alongside a continuation of emergency powers. A further consequence of the continuation of emergency powers is the huge economic bombshell for struggling companies. The majority of companies, especially middle-to-small scale, are already on the cusp of collapse, or have already folded. Some of the larger players are likely to seek State financial intervention. What this means is that an increasing array of major corporate enterprises will come under the jurisdiction of State control, almost as if through the backdoor. This less visible form of biocapitalism forces a shift toward a strengthened State/Governmental control of the social-cultural sphere through such instruments of commercial influence. The private sector once again comes under the umbrella of a globalist agenda through the intermediary of the nation State. This is a trajectory that comes closer to the Chinese model of State intervention into the commercial sector.

Biocapitalism is clearly a force of reckoning that is deeply tied to biopolitics and the new reign of biopower. A global regime is emerging that is constructed from an assemblage of institutions, procedures, orthodox 'knowledge narratives' and enforced by authoritarian measures that are instigated through the police/military complex. The changing biopolitical arena of the 21st century, with its economic biocapitalist agenda, simultaneously implies a rising state of biosecurity, as I discuss in the next chapter.

---

xvi https://www.buzzfeednews.com/article/danvergano/more-coronavirus-pandemics-warning

EIGHT

Biosecurity: the biology of control[i]

'Today it is not the city but rather the camp that is the fundamental biopolitical paradigm of the West.'

Giorgio Agamben

In the previous chapter I noted how there had been a shift from the *disciplinary societies* as described by French philosopher Michel Foucault toward more fluid networks of biopower control. As Foucault had stated, the biopower model functions to rule on death rather than to administer life. The older biopower models focused on the exterior modes of enclosure – school, factory, hospital, prison – whereas what I consider as the new reign of biopower is concerned with gaining access to the interior spaces also. Older exterior institutions (school, factory, etc.) have an expiration date – the human being, in contrast, is an ongoing and continuous 'body' available for generational control. The new regime seeks an ongoing vested interest in the exterior and interior spaces. These are the reconfigured social-body politics of control – or, the *biology of control*. The new reign of biopower is concerned with continual modulation, adapting to the ongoing events more like a fluid network than a fixed institution.

• • • • • • • • • • • • • • • •

i   An earlier version of this chapter first appeared in the magazine 'New Dawn' (no.184 – Jan-Feb 2021)

The 'pandemic era' (as put forth by Fauci and Morens) gives humanity an elusive, ever-present enemy that attacks and infiltrates not only inter-bodily but especially intra-bodily. Human societies exist in open, not closed, systems. As such, the emerging biopower regimes need to gain access through these porous social-body systems. To gain control, they thus need to have proprietary dominion over an individual's body, outside and within. We only have to recognize the rise in molecular engineering, genetic manipulations, and pharmaceutical interventions to see how the external systems have been increasingly gaining interior ground.

It is a tragic fact that humanity has been living amidst a regime of perpetual warfare since known history. From the last 100 years alone, there have been (amongst many others), two World Wars, the Korean War, the Vietnam War, the Cold War, the War on Terror, and now the 'Virus Wars.' In line with the unfolding trend of technology, the 'wars' are shifting from inter-bodies (between bodies) to intra-body (within bodies). The current state of 'perpetual warfare' is attempting to colonize the terrain within our most sacred space – inside of the human biological body. Because of this, humanity has entered a revamped era of biosecurity.

A State of Biosecurity

The biopower politics of 'control over life' backed by technologies of biocapitalism gives rise to draconian measures of State biosecurity. There is no biopolitics which is not simultaneously also a security apparatus. Similarly, there is no biosecurity which is not a systemic form of regulation. State biopower is exercising a corruptive potential to hold human life hostage. This includes the potential of utilizing biosecurity measures to expose and restrain those individuals who make a choice to resist the forces of biopower over their lives.

State institutions across the globe are attempting to define themselves as a sole monopoly in the use of force to ensure biosecurity over the population. Non-state actors are also being brought in as institutionalized, and thus sanctioned, players and actors in this monopoly. Many countries already have their own form of Biosecurity Act in place to deal with the declared 'human biosecurity emergency.' Such a declaration gives the State the authority it needs to enforce its citizens to comply with the emergency requirements. People found engaging in 'contravening behaviour' are likely liable for immediate fines and prison sentences. In the new biosecurity regime, liberty is granted in accordance to rules of 'immunity jurisdiction.' Such jurisdictions are likely to soon include the need for a type of 'immunity passport.' The anticipated immunity passport will create totally reconfigured spaces of mobility and access where travel, public and social events, and state services may be closed to those who, without verified biosecure immunity, are *persona non grata*. As one example, the CommonPass is now being trialled by a small number of passengers flying from the UK to the US.[ii] Travel within nation states and across international boundaries may only become possible through a highly regulated architecture of surveillance and on-body tracking. If a person does not submit their live bio-data, then mobility will be disallowed or highly curtailed. The early signs of this exercise of biosecurity has appeared in States such as Singapore where the tagging of citizens is the first wave of bio-surveillance.[iii]

The new regimes of biopower are establishing continuous variations of 'testing,' with continual iterations of 'being at risk.' If we are to be continually 'at risk,' then we have to be perpetually monitored – the two concepts go hand in hand. And in the present age of heightened mobility, we can expect a fluid 'administration of control' that will

---

ii https://tottnews.com/2020/11/15/commonpass-digital-health-passport/
iii https://21stcenturywire.com/2020/09/23/bio-surveillance-singapore-issuing-bluetooth-tracking-tag-for-citizens/

come through the flows of always-on, surveillant tracking/tracing. 'Track and trace' record keeping has been imposed not only upon the hospitality sectors but also places of worship, businesses, and other organizations. As with risk and monitoring, the tracking goes hand in hand with testing. And in order to undergo testing, people must succumb to giving up their biological data. People's private intra-body data becomes part of the burgeoning biometric data-machine of huge corporations. In an interview with the Wall Street Journal (October 2020), the US administration's appointed 'vaccine czar' – Moncef Slaoui - stated that tech giants Google and Oracle were to 'collect and track vaccine data.'[iv] In a previous interview, Slaoui had referred to this tracking 'data-driven timeline' as a "very active pharmacovigilance surveillance system."[v] This 'on-time' biosecurity testing and tracking will soon be necessary for even the most fundamental acts such as going to a live music concert.

    Ticketmaster, which merged with Live Nation in 2010, to create the music industry's foremost concert promoter and ticket agent, publicly stated in November 2020 that it will check the Covid-19 vaccination status of ticket buyers before issuing passes when live events return in 2021.[vi] It was announced that Ticketmaster has been working on developing what they call a system for 'post-pandemic fan safety' to verify fans' vaccination status or whether they've tested negative for the coronavirus within a 24 to 72 hour window. Ticketmaster is planning on combining the Ticketmaster digital ticket app, third party health information companies like CLEAR Health Pass or IBM's Digital Health Pass, and testing and vaccine distribution providers. When the person receives their test/vaccine certification via

• • • • • • • • • • • • • • • •
iv   https://www.wsj.com/articles/the-captain-of-operation-warp-speed-11602278486
v   https://www.nytimes.com/2020/10/05/opinion/sway-kara-swisher-moncef-slaoui.html?showTranscript=1
vi   https://www.billboard.com/articles/business/touring/9481166/ticketmaster-vaccine-check-concerts-plan/

their 'health pass company,' the health pass would then verify their Covid-19 status to Ticketmaster. If all is 'clean' then Ticketmaster will issue the fan the credentials needed to access the event. On the other hand, if a person tests positive or doesn't have a valid, up-to-date vaccine certificate, they will not be granted access to the event. Ticketmaster president Mark Yovich is on record as stating that he expects the demand for 'digital screening services' will attract a new wave of investors and entrepreneurs to "fuel the growth of a new COVID-19 technology sector" (i.e., biocapitalism). Marianne Herman, co-founder of a company that focuses on assisting entertainment companies develop Covid-19 strategies, stated: "In order for live events to return, technology and science are going to play huge roles in establishing integrated protocols so that fans, artists, and employees feel safe returning to venues."[vii] Welcome to the new biosecurity regime of 'integrated protocols.'

Bio-Control Protocols

Some of the major players in healthcare systems and business have already been getting together to declare what these 'integrated protocols' may likely consist of. The *Riyadh Declaration on Digital Health* was formulated during the Riyadh Global Digital Health Summit, Aug 11–12, 2020. It called itself a 'landmark forum' for highlighting the importance of digital technology, data, and innovation for 'fighting pandemics.' According to their Health Summit webpage:

> It aims to bring together leaders of healthcare systems, public health, digital health, academic institutions and businesses in order to dis-

---

[vii] https://www.billboard.com/articles/business/touring/9481166/ticketmaster-vaccine-check-concerts-plan/

cuss the vital role of digital health in the fight against current and future pandemics.[viii]

The Lancet medical journal did a feature on *The Riyadh Declaration* in which a 'panel of 13 experts' articulated seven key priorities and nine recommendations 'for data and digital health that need to be adopted by the global health community to address the challenges of the COVID-19 pandemic and future pandemics.'[ix] In this, they give the first priority for the health and care sectors to adopt applied health intelligence (HI). What is HI? Apparently, the report says that – 'HI is used for the surveillance, monitoring, and improvement of population and patient outcomes.' The second priority relates to 'interoperable digital technology' and for this technology to be scaled up and sustainable. The third priority is to support the adoption of artificial intelligence (AI). From the nine recommendations, the following are of particular interest: 2) Work with global stakeholders to confront propagation of misinformation or disinformation through social media platforms and mass media; 3) Implement a standard global minimum dataset for public health data reporting; 7) Ensure surveillance systems combine an effective public health response; and 9) Maintain, continue to fund, and innovate surveillance systems as a core component of the connected global health system for rapid preparedness and optimal global responses.

At the very least, these recommendations sound ominously like the framework for establishing a biosecurity apparatus that is a biocapitalist consortium of healthcare businesses, digital health corporations, and state governments. Yet do not think for a moment that the average working person will not need to pay into this apparatus. At the end of 2020, Deutsche Bank researchers proposed a 5% tax for people *choosing* to work from home rather than the office. The reality, as we know, is that many people will not

---

viii https://rgdhs2020.com/
ix https://www.thelancet.com/journals/lancet/article/PIIS0140-6736(20)31978-4/fulltext

be given the choice; yet, as the new report from the German bank says, the average person would be 'no worse off if they paid this tax' because by working remotely 'they save money on travel, food, and clothes.' One of the report's authors (a research strategist at Deutsche Bank) stated that: "Working from home will be part of the 'new normal' well after the pandemic has passed. We argue that remote workers should pay a tax for the privilege...That means remote workers are contributing less to the infrastructure of the economy whilst still receiving its benefits." [x] In other words, within the new biopower regime, people may not be contributing enough 'into the system' if they are working from home – and so must be taxed *for the privilege*. What this shows is that the biology of control, through increased intrusions between human bodies and within them, is a direct curtailing of human sovereignty.

The Question of Human Sovereignty

The new enclosures are no longer disciplinary institutions (as identified by Foucault) but the fluid flows and networks of inter and intra-body spaces and the new regimes that are arising to govern these social-biological terrains. The individual human body has now been more fully incorporated into the global body politique. There are no 'fixed markets' for biopower; instead, there are the flexible networks of exchange and regulation. Yet the question remains – who sets the parameters of legal authority on these exchanges? The world of human civilization has effectively entered the age of the erosion of biological boundaries. Citizens from all backgrounds are being targeted as potential mobile hosts for their own crippling disease - regardless of the true potency of such viruses – just as a person could be a suspicious target in the War on Terror. In both cases, the human being has been re-cast as a site of suspicion and risk. The

---

[x] https://www.businessinsider.com/deutsche-bank-working-from-home-tax-staff-workers-businesses-2020-11

body is now re-classified as a 'site of weakness' – which may itself play into a later transhumanism agenda, as I discuss in Part Three. What is becoming ever clearer is that the new reign of biopower is denying people their rights to keep the frontiers of the human body closed. The fundamental right to health (health safety) is being reconstituted as a legal obligation to health (biosecurity).[xi] This is a process that is both overtly and covertly attempting to reorganize human citizenry in a way that creates maximum obedience to institutions of governance and security. This is also a process that will eventually lead to denying each person their individual sovereignty.

Biosecurity - the *biology of control* - will continue to engage in its newfound power to restructure the totality of social life, and to intrude upon the bodies of the human population as well as upon human consciousness. The danger here is that such draconian strategies go towards enforcing a 'mute life' upon individuals, disallowing them the basic rights of testimony and protest. Such biosecurity measures are nothing less than the power of authoritarian dictatorship operating through the false façade of health and safety. Human biological life is being merged with the physical-digital systems of State biopower to reconfigure not only the cultural narratives but also the very thinking patterns that have constructed many people's belief structures.

A person can be both consciously and unconsciously torn between what they are told to believe and what actually *is*. This can easily create a schism in the human psyche and result in further social divisions and polarizations within familial and cultural groupings. The most common response to anomalous data is to try to fit it into pre-existing parameters of thought – our existing 'reality boxes' - in an attempt to maintain a sense of stability. When the irrational encroaches upon consensus reality, a person is forced to accept the abnormalities as the 'new normal' or to un-

---

xi   See the work of Patrick Zylberman, (Tempêtes microbiennes, Gallimard 2013) dergo critical, and often radical, change at a personal level. Such polarizing events have the result of affecting both the conscious and the unconscious mind. This is not the time to be fostering mental, emotional, and socio-cultural dissociations. The question of human sovereignty applies to each and every person. It is not a privilege or a luxury – it is a basic right and necessity.

The rise of biosecurity amid the converging health intelligence (HI), along with tech-based 'integrated protocols,' and the increased reliance upon Artificial Intelligence both within healthcare systems as well as state-sponsored surveillance, all point towards a worryingly comprehensive 'full spectrum dominance' over human life. It is a biopower-enforced control system not only between bodies and within bodies, but also within the human mind, as I discuss in the following chapter.

NINE

Psycho-Power

*'When we click Like, we are bowing down
to the order of domination.'*

Byung-Chul Han

To frame human life under a reign of comprehensive biopower, the State authorities must also render *conscious life* under its rule. That is, what we 'think' is a part of what we physically 'are' and, as such, is also under their jurisdiction. By literally being born, the State automatically assumes the power to dictate human conscious thinking. From this perspective, it can be seen why current censorship – internet censorship and the curtailing of free speech – has been so dominant and heavy-handed. After all, total power requires total domination. This means not only external control over an individual's body but also to interiorize this control – both mentally (conditioning, programming) and biologically (health treatment, vaccination, etc). As the reign of biopower continues to unfold, people are going to experience many more instances where the *biology of control* situates itself into daily life. It is a calculating narrative because, after all, does not everyone wish for good health and well-being? The situation, however, is being managed and coerced into a state where each person will have no choice over how they make their own health decisions. Biopower forces dominion over external and internal realms through the rhetoric (or double-talk) of representing the *power of well-being*. Yet, the end result is more on the side of *controlling the human being* – and few people, it seems, have an adequate response to this. The very nature of how we recognize human *well-being* is at the core of what is transpiring now in these present times.

Biopower is also, I propose, a control system for human consciousness. This is being verified by the rapid rush into censorship to curb any information that criticizes or is contrary to the consensus programming. The current biological 'state of emergency' is forcing people, on a global scale, to accept previously unimagined ideas to the point where the human psyche is becoming tested to its limits. A new narrative is being established and seeded into mass human consciousness. The replacement 'consensus reality' of the world is attempting to colonize our private senses. It is propagating a new *shared affinity*, of conditioned thought. And yet this is more likely to cause dissonance than cohesion.

The question of freedom, especially freedom of thought, is now bringing forth its own forms of constraint, and generating new forms of coercion. German–Korean philosopher Byung-Chul Han has stated that the new form of power of post-industrial capitalism is a form of *psycho-politics*. Psycho-politics implies that those who are being ruled think they are acting freely, but they are acting the way that those who are in charge want. This ruling exploits the freedom of the individual and makes them choose the most convenient choice for the ruler through a precise control of the psyche. In other words, we have entered the phase of auto-exploitation where people have allowed themselves to be exploited by themselves. In turn, we direct our aggression back against ourselves because, as Han notes, people are less liable to revolt when they are depressed: 'Psychic maladies such as depression and burnout express a profound crisis of freedom. They represent pathological signs that freedom is now switching over into manifold forms of compulsion.'[1] Whilst previous forms of existing biopower did not overtly intervene into the human psyche, it did prepare the groundwork for the newly emerging biology of control to gain influence over the *intra-space* of the human psyche.

As discussed, when biopower emerged in the institutions of the 18th century, and onwards, it represented the shift from Sovereign 'royal power' to disciplinary power following the transition from agrarian to industrial life. Industrialization necessitated a form of bodily discipline to adapt it to a form of machinic production. Now that we are transitioning from industrial to digital life, power is no longer over the 'docile body' but over the intra-body - the genetic, cellular life – as well as *conscious life*. Disciplinary power is about training the body, subjecting it to drills and rules. Now, however, the 'docile body' must also incorporate the 'docile psyche' - not only to reach into the biological body but to invade, influence, and steer the psyches of the population. The new reign of biopower that is attempting to secure its dominion is a combination of a carefully controlled 'administration of bodies,' a calculated 'management of life,' and a persistent 'programming of consciousness.' In the words of Jose Delgado, a professor of neurophysiology at Yale University and a famed mind control researcher: we are shifting into a *psychocivilized* society. In psycho-power, the human *being* is the site of target, including their conscious and unconscious thought patterns.

It should be clear by now that the new forms of modern governance that are being put into place will manage and exploit a 'psycho-power' technology of domination. Philosopher Byung-Chul Han agrees that this will constitute a new form of *psycho-governance*. That is, governance will be imposed not only from the traditional nation state body but more so through technologies of influencing the human mind and how people think. This system of *psycho-power* will employ digital technologies, and the digital-surveillance space, as its dominant, pervasive medium of control. It is here where power relations are interiorized within the individual, and falsely interpreted as freedom. Rather than pulling ourselves up by the bootstraps, we are chaining ourselves through the psyche.

Further, psycho-power is not about controlling the past but about manipulating the memories of it so that the present can be forged anew. The new reality consensus is almost erasing the pre-pandemic past. We can sense this already occurring. The world-before-2020 now seems like a bygone age. It is surprising too how many people have readily accustomed themselves to this 'new normal' way of life with its biosecurity regulations. Another point to recognize is that within this new biopower reign, emotions are actively encouraged and often deliberately targeted and heightened. This is in contradistinction to within earlier disciplinary societies where emotions were considered as distractions from an orderly and mechanical functioning. Yet the new 'Fourth Industrial Revolution,' as the World Economic Forum labels it, is about a new functionality – a digitally-managed gameboard of disruption, diversion, and entanglement simultaneously. As part of this increased emotional engagement, certain 'technologies of the self' are promoted.

With more and more people set to be working from home, we can only imagine how practices for 'self-optimization' are going to be peddled even more than previously. These may include online motivational retreats, management workshops, personality seminars, etc., - all forms of self-optimization in order to better operate within the system. And within such a system, points of weakness are to be worked on in order to gain increased 'efficiency and performance.' Yet we would do well to remember that the 'good self' is not the same as living the 'good life.' It is more likely that the 'good self' is the slave to the system - the system of *psycho-power*. It is a system that has shown not only a willingness but a determination to exploit the increasingly consumerist 'consciousness industry.' Being hooked onto the 'positive thinking' teachings may actually distract a person from doing deeper interior examination of themselves.

In other words, being positive about self-optimization can become a retreat from the real work a person needs to engage with. As Han has also recognized, constantly working at the self-improvement industry can become a new form of work ethic: 'Now, instead of searching out sins, one hunts down negative thoughts.'[2]

Italian philosopher Franco Berardi takes an even stronger position. In his perspective, a new fascism is arising: '...the new fascism that results from the implosion of desire, from the attempt to keep panic under control and from the depressive rage of impotence.'[3] The once prevalent *will to power*, he says, has now been replaced by an impotent rage. Berardi sees that a psychopharmacological addiction and disorientation is the new despondency - a form of aggressive self-contempt amid mental mayhem within which resides an impotent desire for revenge. And yet, the new fluid spaces are making any real responses invalid and impotent: 'Social life has been pulverized in the metropolitan, post-political, deterritorialized space, and potency is but a myth, a counterpoint to present impotence.'[4] It may be a sign of painful irony that in an age of impotence, as Berardi calls it, human fertility is rapidly declining.

In such times as these, the burning questions come back to us about the fundamentals of human life – *what is a 'human life'?*

What is a Human Life?

The 'Covid Event 2020' is in danger of providing the globalist agenda with its great coup over the management of consensus reality. This *perception intervention* may have provided the final stimulus necessary to tip the twenty-first century into an awaiting technologically manipulated reality. A new landscape is emerging where, for the first time, the human body is finding itself out-of-place and vulnerable within its own territory. What are now being regarded as the emerging 'post-pandemic' landscapes are likely to be uncomfortable territory for our mental, emotional, and physical states. The human condition is under further, accelerated, modification.

The world is moving perilously toward a recombinant future where, in the words of one tech CEO, 'Humans are biohazards, machines are not.'[i] The citizen is now subjected to an external authority in ways that never before could be achieved. The new reign of biopower is reconstituting how humans are being targeted as objects – or 'units' – to be controlled, with our bodies as well as our minds as the new colonies to be conquered. The peril facing the future of human civilization upon this planet is whether humanity as we know it will form the core body and/or intelligence of this future. Or will humanity become as manageable and docile 'units' under a digitally-managed biopower regime?

Does this mean that the only way to be exempt from such a comprehensive and pervasive regime is to renounce one's citizenship - to be a 'non-citizen'? Could such a stateless place exist in the contemporary world? Will this trigger the rise of new people's republics? In the light of recent events, we are compelled to ask the question – *what is an authentic human?* Is it possible to live *authentically* when subjected to the external power regimes of authority that deny a person their individual sovereignty? The politics of life are fast being used against the masses in order to develop the *docile bodies* that the globalist 'Great Reset' agenda seeks in order to roll out its technocratic future. It is no overstatement to say that the future of humanity is on the table. How the next years unfold will determine not only the direction of our human future but also, importantly, *how* human our future will be. As a human family it seems some have forgotten the Hippocratic oath that states: 'Neither will I administer a poison to anybody when asked to do so, nor will I suggest such a course.' The very politics of life

---

i https://theintercept.com/2020/05/08/andrew-cuomo-eric-schmidt-coronavirus-tech-shock-doctrine/

(and death) are being usurped for an agenda that shows little, if no, human compassion and fellowship. State biopower is concerned with power *over* life rather than life itself. And it is this that makes it profoundly disturbing and of great danger to a human-based future. The new biopower regimes, and their attendant biology of control, may speak of renewal and recalibration yet it speaks of an age that is void of the very core qualities of being human in a living, organic world. As individuals, we also have a very real human power residing within us. Each one of us is now being asked to face this central question: What does being human mean to me, and what is true human freedom?

TEN

Unfreedom Narratives: the new states of exception

'A comfortable, smooth, reasonable, democratic unfreedom prevails in advanced industrial civilization, a token of technical progress.'

Herbert Marcuse

The Universal Declaration of Human Rights contains thirty articles. Nine of those articles directly state the word 'freedom.' We therefore expect that a range of freedoms are our basic human rights. We consider ourselves as 'free' and independent individuals. The shift into the 'modern era' was considered as a move into a world where calamity and catastrophic disasters would be put to rest. Yet, on the contrary, rather than modern life extinguishing the presence of existential threats it has increased them. And the latest threat to have arrived, post-War on Terror, is of the biological kind. An almost pervasive presence of underlying 'civilized fears' now exist to further modify human behavior and thought. And like bedfellows, freedom, risk, and fear often walk hand in hand. Risks are considered as calculable dangers where we at least have some capacity to calculate their potential. But modern risks are that which we can neither predict nor fully escape from because they flirt too close to our dark fantasies. Whereas risks can be seen as *ex*plosions, emanating from without, our fears are the *im-*

plosions that erupt from within – such as the fear of viruses. And since we cannot relieve ourselves of risk, and their attendant fear, then a state of unfreedom perpetuates itself.

The German-born philosopher and social psychologist Erich Fromm spent most of his life trying to understand freedom in relation to the human condition. He came to the conclusion that only a fundamental change in our character, in the way we do things, will save us from a psychological and economic disaster. He saw clearly what was on the cards if human nature was to continue along the same lines, and without making a change in its current course. The modern person, suggested Fromm, is afraid to lose their sense of identity. Any form of drastic social change spells a break-up of many incumbent social norms upon which their social persona – i.e., identity – is constructed. What many people still fail to realize is that the social persona – a person's character - is a social construct formed out of a sophisticated and complex array of cultural conditioning and programming. What the average person fears to lose is the artificial 'sense of self' which has been grafted onto them through years of socialization. It is thus a false fear – yet a fear all the same. This distinction, between a person's social persona and their genuine self, forms a site of contradiction and contestation that is at the base of much social fragmentation.

Fromm's book *Fear of Freedom* (1941 – published in US as *Escape from Freedom*) put forth the idea that a struggle for freedom had been created between the interior world of an individual and external institutions and systems. The personal fear of social isolation and uncertainty is thus eliminated by seeking an outside power to give their power and dependency to. Eventually, a person becomes an instrument in the hands of structures, institutions, and forms of power external to them. The only other alternative is to seek a form of self-independence based on personal trust and belief. Yet such self-beliefs are constantly undermined by authoritative institutions in the modern world. In this respect, Fromm says that when an individual attempts to become more independent and self-reliant, they also become more isolated from their social systems, and this can create fear of isolation. In a similar manner, the new consensus reality being established is attempting to strengthen this dependency upon external systems – through the fear of biosecurity. This dependency is either being compelled upon people through triggering their own fears (through heightened narratives of risk); or they are being enforced upon people through regimes of biopower.

As was noted during the lockdowns of 2020, many people found it difficult to be forced into the enclosed spaces of their homes and cut-off from social engagements and networks. The covid-19 pandemic response made it obligatory for millions of people across the globe to experience 'self-isolation,' which proved difficult for those not used to such ways of unfreedom. This caused great personal unrest and psychological discomfort as so many people have been conditioned to a life of exterior distraction and mobility. Further, it showed that people have unconscious fears about freedom and risk. We are fascinated, noted Fromm, by the wielding of powers *outside* ourselves yet are blinded to the condition of our own *inner* restraints in the form of compulsions and fears. It is these individual and social conditions that make for the suppression of human life and its proclivity for control and management.

In his *Fear of Freedom*, Fromm proposes that our inherent – and often unrecognized – fear of personal freedom and self-independence, results in the following escape mechanisms:

- *Automaton conformity*: changing one's ideal self to conform to a perception of society's preferred type of personality, losing one's true self in the process; *Automaton conformity* displaces the burden of choice from self to society.

- *Authoritarianism*: giving control of oneself to another. By submitting one's freedom to someone else, this act removes the freedom of choice almost entirely.

- *Destructiveness*: any process which attempts to eliminate others or the world as a whole, all to escape freedom.[1]

Fromm saw that a collective form of 'destruction of the world' was a last, desperate attempt by people as a way to save themselves being crushed by their unprocessed fears. In a stark yet highly prescient observation, he wrote: 'Because we have freed ourselves of the older overt forms of authority, we do not see that we have become the prey of a new kind of authority. We have become automatons who live under the illusion of being self-willing individuals.'[2] It is a major statement to recognize that the new kind of authority people place themselves under comes from their own compliance. It is a form of unfreedom willingly accepted because most people 'believe' that they already have freedom as 'self-willing individuals.' Yet the contrary is more likely – that people behave as automatons because they are complying with society's consensus narrative. This is what Fromm refers to as *automaton conformity*. Further, that this conformity is just one aspect in the bigger picture of submitting one's freedom by outsourcing dependency to an external source, which Fromm notes leads to the condition of *authoritarianism*.

Fromm made an interesting observation in his *Fear of Freedom* by saying that the human being is not really in control of their world but, on the contrary, the artificial structure they helped to construct – what I refer to as the 'modern power machine' – is in fact controlling the human being. Fromm perceptively remarked that,

> The outer chains have simply been put inside of man. The desires and thoughts that the

> suggestion-apparatus of society fills him with, chain him more thoroughly than outer chains. This is so because man can at least be aware of outer chains but be unaware of inner chains, carrying them with the illusion that he is free. He can try to overthrow the outer chains, but how can he rid himself of chains of whose existence he is unaware?[3]

As Herbert Marcuse stated, in the opening citation of this chapter, our unfreedoms come to us as democratically comfortable, smooth, and reasonable. For this reason, most people hardly notice how our freedoms (or lack of them) are tied into the 'power machine' of the system.

The fears that correspond to our freedoms are related to the condition of risk prevalent in our societies at any given time. And risks, especially biological risks, are now being planted as the potential bogeymen within everyday life. French sociologist Hugues Lagrange, in his study of fear, came to term as 'derivative fear' that which guides much of modern behavior. It acts as a secondary type of fear when there isn't any immediate threat present. It is a sediment, a residue, that outlives any *actual* threat; somehow the shadow of the menace lingers on, haunting us. It shapes our behavior regardless of whether any direct threat to us exists. It is this type of fear that can be easily planted within the potential for lurking pandemics.

This lingering type of fear is more intangible, invisible, and hence cannot be quantified or reasonably assessed by us. It makes people more susceptible and vulnerable to feelings of insecurity and disempowerment. We are open to attack, to risk of infection, at any time; we are instilled with a lack of trust. And, importantly, we are more willing to obey (i.e., willing obedience) to those authoritative powers that promise defense and security. Any person who has internalized the sense emotions of derivative fear will be more willing to respond as if to threat even in the absence of a genuine threat. Such behavior is self-managed and is exactly what the reign of biopower seeks. Those individuals in so-called 'developed' territories live in some of the most secured societies, pampered with consumerism and entertainment, and yet feel the most threatened, insecure, vulnerable, and liable to panic than most other societies.

As seen during 2020, this internal fear of infection has made it possible for external actors to intervene in our private lives, even without permission. People are fear-driven to give away their freedom to others. As film-maker Adam Curtis said: 'In an age when all the grand ideas have lost credibility, fear of a phantom enemy is all the politicians have left to maintain their power.'[4] We are then offered their 'new securities' in the form of democratic unfreedoms.

Unfreedoms & (In)Securities

The 'new normal' of the consensus reality now in-formation is attempting to impose a manageable control over 'unruly social chaos' and risk uncertainties. Today, the reality is that power and politics have now split apart. Power is no longer truly exercised through the façade of political institutions - it has shifted into an extraterritorial space that is beyond boundaries, nations, laws, visibility, and accountability. External power is now invisible, intangible, and almost ethereal. The need for security, which is being rolled out as a social stabilizing force, is yet another form of power. Yet it is utilizing the same strategies that have been present throughout most of human history: the people give their cooperation to be ruled, and this is welcomed by the rulers. Again, citing Marcuse – *'Free election of masters does not abolish the masters or the slaves.'* It is this compliant agreement that sustains authority. Social management is a mix of external persuasion and our own complicit self-surveillance. As philosopher Jean-Pierre Dupuy observes, 'We are condemned to perpetual vigilance.'[5]

Insecurities are now becoming the norm of today's increasingly securitized societies. Insecurity has insinuated itself into our social and political configurations. In other words, (in)security is now systemic; but it is far from static. Earlier dystopic visions of (in)security, notably from Orwell and Huxley, regarded such cultures as being more solidified. Security and power/control regimes were well-positioned and intimidating. Or, in Huxley's case, they were engrained within our compelling pleasures. Today, (in)securities and regimes of power and control are fluid, uncertain, non-visible, and constantly on the move; they adapt, re-position, and re-configure themselves. In return, 'we the people' often define ourselves against such threats as a way of being seen as apart from them: 'We all need to mark the enemies of security in order to *avoid being counted among them*...We need to accuse in order to be absolved; to exclude in order to avoid exclusion.'[6]

Exclusion now forms a major aspect in the reign of biopower under discussion. As in the theme of disease, there is the division between the 'infected' and the 'healthy,' and this is being exacerbated by the arrival of health passes, as mentioned. The desire for safety, says Italian philosopher Giorgio Agamben, is creating what he refers to as a 'state of exception.' In an online essay, posted 26th February 2020, he reflects upon the government's restrictions upon freedom:

> 'The other factor, no less disquieting, is the state of fear, which in recent years has diffused into individual consciousnesses and which translates into a real need for states of collective panic, for which the epidemic once again offers the ideal pretext. Therefore, in a perverse vicious circle, the limitation of freedom imposed by governments is accepted in the name of a desire for safety, which has been created by the same governments who now intervene to satisfy it.'[i]

••••••••••••••••
i   http://positionspolitics.org/giorgio-agamben-the-state-of-exception-provoked-by-an-unmotivated-emergency/

What is manifesting here is the growing tendency to use the state of exception as a normal governing paradigm. In the end, such securitized 'states of exception' generate increased insecurity, either as a by-product or perhaps as a deliberate in-built policy. This then fosters a 'security anxiety' where many people are encouraged to respond to the new insecurities by adopting ever-greater external security measures. The public collective mindset is further conditioned with feelings of insecurity that are then strengthened with relentless repetition by politicians and the media. Insecurity begets increased security – it is a self-fulfilling cycle. We almost seem to forget that the state of being *in security* needs our willing compliance.

The concept of biosecurity in our current societies is being reinforced through biopower strategies that are implementing new regimes of order, control, and unfreedom. To not have these, we are being told, will lead to a breakdown in security and collective well-being, leading to chaos and disorder. Within our highly complex and diverse cultures, the threat of chaos and disruption is usually enough to gain support for restrictive security measures. Erich Fromm was prescient in recognizing that a hugely influential, almost secret, power is exercised over the whole of society in a way that conditions not only our ways of thinking but also how we perceive reality. Human reality has been hijacked for a long time.

The peril of the moment is that many people continue to live under the illusion of being self-willing individuals. And yet, despite this, every individual has personal agency and the power of sovereignty. However, we can only perceive this if we can extricate ourselves from the emerging new consensus reality that incorporates biopower, biosecurity, and increasing narratives of unfreedom. New landscapes are quickly forming, bringing with them their readapted organization of control. And with such control structures also arise the organization of behavior modification.

ELEVEN

New Landscapes: the organization of behaviour modification

'Everyone who had ever lived was literally surrounded by the iron walls of the prison; they were all inside it and none of them knew it.'

Philip K. Dick

Social organization has invariably, from earliest times, also been about control. The organization of people and society goes together with issues of social management and structures of control. This is neither an obscure nor hidden fact. Every time you walk into a building, whether it is a supermarket, an office, a residential block, your movement is being managed according to the layout of the building. In other words, physical structures by necessity organize (and thus, control) the movement of bodies. Yet this is not the same as deeply employed and sustained deliberate control measures through a combination of physical-digital 'architectures of oppression' (as Edward Snowden remarked). Behaviour regulation as tied to structures and institutions was made into public discussion most notably by the research of Michel Foucault. More recently, social theorist Michalis Lianos has stated that 'institutional control is not spontaneous as is the case in social communities. It is produced as a planned *managerial* activity corresponding to the complex mode of organisation of contemporary Western society.'[1] As Lianos also notes, institutional control can be considered beneficial since it orders and protects our social needs. This is because it is often functioning free from an overarching agenda and serves only to provide efficiency of use. However, institutional control has now merged with technological architectures and these have been implanted with attached agendas. Technological neutrality is not possible as any technology (or tool) has its influence and impact upon human life. And these influences and impacts have dramatically increased with the arrival of digital technologies, as most of us have already experienced. Digital technologies especially are affecting the human psyche, more so when implemented as part of the system of psycho-power.

Technological systems are increasingly embedded into our environments as deliberate social management driven agendas. These, I suggest, are forming the new landscapes of behaviour modification. The inertia that many social theorists thought attached to technology is no longer applicable. Technologies are increasingly operated and implemented by those with specific motivations and agendas. It is no longer possible to consider technological systems solely with regard to their 'operational' or 'quantitative' potential. Modern human societies and cultures have replaced those earlier ordering technologies/tools with devices and techno-systems that now rule over our minds. Human perceptions, free will, and freedoms are now being managed within grand architectures of control. These new landscapes are impacting the human psyche and attempting to forge a new reality perception. The technologies that now face us have clear features: information control, physical-mobility regulation, and control over human perception.

The most recent forms of power-management are being presented as health security – *biosecurity* - that are re-structuring our landscapes: lifestyles, city life, the office and workspaces, physical and digital movements, and more. The modification of these spaces is set to further desensitize people to the ongoing regulation of their movements – specifically, the increased constriction of 'human' spaces. The new consensus reality is also about a reconfiguration of spatial territories. The post-pandemic landscape is merging physical-digital spaces into new corridors of permitted human contact. This restructuring is sure to affect (or 'infect'?) the human psyche. The Italian philosopher Franco Berardi has noted that our electronic and digital environments are putting 'the sensitive organism in a state of permanent electrocution.'[2] The social-cultural body is being deliberately targeted by strategies that cause anxiety, fragmentation, exhaustion, confusion, polarization, and fear. These have been implemented through a wave of continual national and local lockdowns; social restrictions; loss of human interaction; anti-social forms of ostracization; loss of economic independence, and more. The human condition is being subjected to a new rhythm of the modern power-machine that is breaking down accustomed, and necessary, social alliances.

The established conditions that created a prior sense of social reality are being dissolved and replaced with processes aimed at managing the masses through forms of separation and quantification. That is, with the techniques necessary to begin the formation of a technologized humanity. These processes seek to reduce human life, and its environment, to something measurable and predicable - a life ordained by algorithms. These imposed changes are creating a disequilibrium in the human psyche – a fragmentation of the human self. Furthermore, such strategies seek to break down trusted social relations and render people more digitally dependent. As a conscious, biological organism we are being prepared to mimic the automation of the machine. Humanity is being cleverly coerced into an awaiting future where the human, social collective is physically distanced, digitally monitored, and regimented through modalities of biosecurity.

Techniques have been devised, and already employed, to produce normalized and standardized behaviour in order to create a socially managed populace. The collective human mind is being adopted and adapted into an infrastructure of control that operates largely through modes of digital connectivity that exerts control over human expression and autonomy of behaviour. To enact this, a consortium of institutions have been selected to structure contemporary societies toward specific functions that give the promise of security and human well-being whilst developing increased social dependency. This is the post-pandemic landscape now rapidly arising and to which all future generations shall be born into. Such new landscapes shall manage us from cradle to grave.

The City as Machine Cradle

Modern living, especially within dense urban metropolises, as well as within poverty-stricken neighbourhoods, severely affects the human psychological condition, as well as affecting the nervous system. Journalist Naomi Klein has noted how a form of 'Pandemic Shock Doctrine' is emerging where city metropolises are forming suspicious partnerships with large tech conglomerates to re-design city living. Klein has stated that the quarantine lockdowns were not so much to save lives 'but as a living laboratory for a permanent — and highly profitable — no-touch future.'[3] One tech CEO that Klein interviewed commented that: 'There has been a distinct warming up to human-less, contactless technology…Humans are biohazards, machines are not.'[4] Several local city governments are in negotiations with large private tech companies to create a 'seamless integration' between city government, education, health, and policing operations. Further, the individual home will become a smart-enclosed hub for the urban dweller. All this, and more, as a 'frontline pandemic response.'

Online learning, the home office, telehealth, and online commerce are all now a part of an emerging investment landscape to convert existing physical-digital infrastructures to cloud-based ones that will be incorporated into the coming fully completed 5G network. All in the name of providing citizens with a securitized 'virus free' landscape. Erich Schmidt, ex-CEO of Google/Alphabet and now chair of the Defense Innovation Board that advises the US Department of Defense on military A.I., announced publicly:

> 'The benefit of these corporations, which we love to malign, in terms of the ability to communicate, the ability to deal with health, the ability to get information, is profound. Think about what your life would be like in America without Amazon.'[5]

Schmidt has now been hired to head up the task force commissioned to reimagine New York's post-Covid reality. And he isn't alone. High-tech is now jumping to get into partnerships with local governments in order to bring a safer, more 'securitized' landscape into civil society – for the benefit of all.

The business office landscape is also under re-organization to further regulate the social interactions of working colleagues. It is clear from the announcements thus far that a new form of business behaviour modification is in the works. In a recent business analysis published in Bloomberg, it was suggested that:

> The pre-Covid workplace, with its shared desks and common areas designed for "creative collisions," is getting a makeover for the social distancing era. So far, what employers have come up with is a mash-up of airport security style entrance protocols and surveillance combined with precautions already seen at grocery stores, like sneeze guards and partitions.[6]

The authors of the report also foresee that the newly returned office worker will likely be encased in a makeshift cubicle made of plexiglass sheets. A mode of employee anti-interaction is clearly a new trend in office design.

Hundreds of major companies, at least, are planning what they call 'employee re-orientation programs' and have already hired 'thermal scanners' to monitor employees for fevers, according to the business analysis report. The report also stated that there has been a spike in job postings for 'tracers,' who would track down the contacts of anyone who tests positive for the covid-19 virus. In short, companies are now looking for a range of solutions to keep people away from one another throughout the working day. IBM, for example, is looking into using existing sensors or finding new technology to detect when people are too close together or 'trending' in that direction. Another report from the UK[i] noted how companies were looking into developing their own specialist employee smartphone apps that would operate elevators hands-free. The language employers are using includes creating 'safe bubbles' around employees and monitoring so that these 'safe bubbles' do not overlap. Technologies and techniques for office monitoring is now big business and can be viewed as an indirect yet related part of the burgeoning biocapitalism market.

Various companies, the UK report goes on to say, are looking to teach artificial intelligence (AI) to monitor the video cameras that are monitoring the employees. The chief technology officer at Motorola Solutions (based in Boston) explained that AI algorithms can offer feedback about 'pinch points' where people are too close together. Instead of employers (read 'humans') having to spend time (read 'waste time') watching the actual video, they can 'ask' the AI how well social distancing is being observed overall,

---

i   See – 'Horrible' offices look to tempt back workers - https://www.bbc.com/news/business-53056585

and where problem points are.[ii] So that's the issue solved then. We will just rely on AI algorithms to tell us how to 'social distance' in our non-interacting bubbles and we can modify our behaviour accordingly. Job done!

What this also signifies is that to be able to modify our behaviour, machine intelligence will need to gather ever greater datasets about us. That is, 'smart cities' and 'secure offices' equals increased surveillance which equals expanded datasets. Today's data is the modern equivalent of the science of statistics from the 18th century that started a euphoric wave as a new form of order, management, and control of knowledge, people, and society. Data is yet another advancement upon the tools to establish control over the masses. The collection, analysis, and interpretation of information about people only results in systems that seek to categorize individuals in restricted ways so that they can be more measurable, knowable, and thus predicted. The philosopher Byung-Chul Han views this rise of 'dataism' as creating a pressure, or compulsion, to conform, and any deviance from 'the norm' is not tolerated. Data, says Han, creates a collective patterning of familiarity - a 'hypertrophied sameness'[7] Such dataism, according to Han, is a short step away from digital totalitarianism, which needs to be recognized for what it is: 'Therefore, a *third Enlightenment* is called for - in order to shine a light on how digital enlightenment has transformed into a new kind of servitude.'[8]

Through the advancement of dataism and operations of technocratic 'normalization,' the modern power-machine age is manufacturing a new standardization of the human body and mind. Socially managed interventions, as well as programmed narratives, are seeking to make people increasingly question the concept of the human self. The human sense of 'self' and identity has become a fragile thing; it is analysed, scrutinized, and criticized through social media; it is modified through surveillance capitalism; and it is increasingly being rendered by AI facial recogni-

---

ii   ibid

tion systems. As these post-pandemic landscapes become increasingly rolled out in more social environments, we are likely to see an ever-greater fragmentation of the human self and destabilizing narratives over the future of the human body (see Part Three). The 'Black Iron Prison' that Philip K. Dick saw coming is now hitting us squarely in the form of totalitarian techno-surveillance.

As I shall discuss further in Part Three, technologies are becoming embedded as living elements within the evolutionary directionality of human life. That is, there is an evident agenda to merge technology within the next phase of human evolution. Technology is no longer merely 'operational' – it is becoming a 'smart' ecosystem merging with human civilization. Philosopher Franco Berardi refers to this merging as a 'techno-media complex' that is now controlling a global 'hyper-connected mind.' Further, Berardi believes that technological advancement and consciousness has now separated: 'As a result, technology has increasing power over social life, while society has decreasing power over technology, and is no more able to govern itself.'[9] This discrepancy, or widening gulf, between the capacity of the human mind (consciousness) to comprehend the role – or 'agendas' – of technology is what Berardi considers to be a looming danger:

> The convergence between the automation of the technical operation and the crumbling of the social mind - depression, despair, aggressiveness, fascism - is the dangerous core of the apparently unstoppable apocalypse that looms on the horizon.[10]

This ominous mix of a 'crumbling' social mind and the rise of automation is what Berardi sees as creating a 'deterritorialized territory empty of real life, in which simulations can freely proliferate, and bodily impurity has to be removed together...'[11] Bodily impurity may soon become another main narrative as the consensus reality presents an organic biological humanity in fear over its *weak bodies*. The human race has arrived to where it is now perilously close to losing the debate on its bodily futures.

PART THREE

Bodily Futures

TWELVE

Weak Bodies

*'Dementia of the body and automation of the brain:
this is the neuro-totalitarian fabric of the Empire of chaos.'*

Franco 'Bifo' Berardi

Erich Fromm, as a psychoanalyst, suggested that human dependency begins with the helplessness of being born and needing extra-long dependency and protection. Our human biological weakness, he says, is the very condition of human culture. The result is that there remains a lifelong struggle between the individual self and those over-whelming strong powers external to us. I would say this situation has now accelerated and shifted so that the struggle is now between the organic body itself and the external forces that seek ever greater merging with technological structures and systems. The biological 'weakness' of the human body is a dangerous narrative that has sprung into the mainstream due to the 2020 pandemic.

As I have discussed, the rising biopower narratives are placing the human physical body as a site of risk. It is vulnerable to the increasing potency of viral infections and nasty contagions. It is not a safe area to be. And yet we are living *within* these zones – quite literally. We inhabit these biological bodies and yet we are being increasingly presented with narratives about their vulnerabilities and weaknesses. I find these narratives worrying as they appear to be as Trojan horses carrying a far more dangerous enemy within their underbelly. That is, they are the early wave carriers of an agenda to persuade/compel humanity towards a transhumanist future. The future of humanity, they are saying, cannot be built upon a foundation of *weak bodies*. The relations between technology and organic life are being rapidly reprogrammed. If anything, the years ahead may be considered as part of an evolutionary mutation as the bio-digital ecosystems merge further. There is a significant chance that the mutation underway may alter the very definition of what it means to be human. Are we on the threshold of homo sapiens becoming Robosapiens? According to some accounts, this may well be the case. The human environment, after all, has always been one of mutational change.

It took millennia for human cultures to shift from the oral traditions into the alphabetical forms, then handwritten onto papyruses and scrolls by dedicated scribes. After this arrived the mechanical arts, from the printing press to the telegraph, and then to the cabled telephone. Now, human culture has taken relatively little evolutionary time to jump into the digital infosphere that combines sensory (visual and tactile) with cognitive (brain patterns) in new modes of interaction. These new forms of interaction will have transformative implications for our social behaviour and psychological patterning. The very fabric of human experience is set to undergo a radical transformation as we begin to lose grip upon the rigidity of our biological form. We are moving away from a domain that has shaped the understanding of the human condition for thousands of years. According to philosopher Franco Berardi, this transition is already well underway and has begun with the externalization of many of our cognitive functions:

> The separation of the brain from the body is the overall effect of this double movement: the brain - the financial brain, the networked brain, the automated brain - is getting con-

nected in a space that is increasingly secluded from the concrete life of the social body, and therefore inaccessible to the action of human beings.[1]

The 'social body' is no longer tied to the individual body – it is 'inaccessible' to us as human beings for the social body has become too automated. Berardi says that the solution to this may be for us to 'make friends' with the automation:

> The automaton is growing in interconnectedness and pervasiveness: the brain has been objectified in the computational machine, then separated from the social body, so the social body seems unable to behave in a meaningful way. The solution for humans is to make friends with the automaton.[2]

This loss of the organic is what Berardi refers to in the opening quote to this chapter as the 'dementia of the body' and the 'automation of the brain,' which he believes is the 'neuro-totalitarian fabric' of the societies that are to come. I address this subject further in the following chapter.

The increasing automation of the world appears to follow an agenda to establish a new form of ecology – a physical-digital hybrid. In this merging, humans will be forced to acknowledge that algorithms and intelligent software will soon, if they are not already, be running nearly everything in our daily lives. Historian Yuval Harari believes that the twenty-first century will be dominated by algorithms. He states that: '"Algorithm" is arguably the single most important concept in our world. If we want to understand our life and our future, we should make every effort to understand what an algorithm is.'[3] Algorithms already follow our shopping habits, recommend products for us, pattern recognize our online behaviour, help us drive our cars, fly our planes, trade our economies, coordinate our public transport, organize our energy distribution, and a lot, lot more that we are not aware of. One of the signs of the loss of the organic is that we are surrounded by an invisible coded environment, written in languages we don't understand. The environments through which humans move are being transformed into what cultural historian Langdon Winner termed 'concealed electronic complexity.'

The rapidly expanding Internet of Things (IoT) will further merge with 5G networks to establish a new 'social body' that will not be organic. Researcher Philip Howard refers to this as a global *Pax Technica* – a world that will operate through a new language. Berardi too notes that such infrastructure will necessitate a form of techno-linguistic automatism. What will become of the human body when its physical representation becomes dispersed into 'digital points of place' without solid human alliances or relations? Will the global infrastructure of human civilization be run on algorithmic logic and techno-abstraction? Berardi believes that 'the techno-linguistic apparatus is taking over the control of the planet' and creating 'a deterritorialized territory empty of real life' where 'bodily impurity has to be removed together.'[4]

This vision is a form of Neo-Gnosticism where human nature is something imperfect or incomplete that has to be enhanced by human selection or machine-hybridisation (e.g., in vitro fertilization, eugenics, or cyborgs). This Neo-Gnostic vision has been with us for a long time and the potential *Robosapien* has its ancestor in the creature of the golem. The golem legend speaks of a creature fashioned from clay, a Cabbalistic motif which has appeared frequently in literary and cinematic form. The Cabbalistic automaton that is the golem, which means 'unformed,' has often been used in cinema to show the struggle between mechanical limitation and human feelings. This struggle depicts the tension that combines cogs and consciousness; the entrapment in matter and the spirit of redemption and liberation. One of the most famous of the golem legends is the one associated with Rabbi Loew of seventeenth-century Prague who created his creature from clay mud of the local Vltava river to protect his people. Soon his very own creation grows in strength and threatens his creator, and so Rabbi Loew reverses his magic spell and returns the creature to dust. Frankenstein is a later western retelling of the golem myth. This is a myth that speaks of the hubris in humanity fashioning its own creatures and 'magically' bestowing life upon them. It is the act of creating a 'sacred machine' from the parts and pieces of a material world and then to imbue them with human traits. And through this human likeness they are required to fulfil human chores and work as slaves. The Cabbalistic humanoid – the sentient robot – is forever doomed, similar to what the new narratives are now saying about humanity being trapped within the confines and limitations of a material reality.

Cinematic explorations of this theme include *Blade Runner*, *Robocop*, *A.I.*, and *Bicentennial Man*, amongst many others. Both *Blade Runner* and *Robocop* depict a human world of violence and the need to create a sentient creature for protection and service; whilst *A.I.* and *Bicentennial Man* demonstrate the wish to create out of emotion and feelings. Running through all these cinematic portrayals is the clash of natures between the human and the non-human. In *Blade Runner* (1982) the major conflict is between Roy (the Replicant – played by Rutger Hauer) and Deckard (the one who hunts down rogue Replicants – played by Harrison Ford). Within this interplay there are constant questions raised as to what constitutes conscious life, as often the poles are turned showing the Replicants as more human than Deckard, the supposed human hunter. Finally, we are left with the ambiguous notion that Deckard might himself unknowingly be a Replicant, implanted with false memories. This idea mirrors the motif that we harbour a wish, a dream, to fashion something pure and yet the error is always that our human traits end up within our own creations. This reflects elements of the Cabbalistic belief in the urge to transcend corrupt matter through realizing the perfect human. And yet, as these films show, there are dangers in blurring the lines between human and automation. Our material reality may be the ultimate *unreal machine*. We are the cogs, the clay golem, the imperfect creature fashioned by another. Our human fears of automation may only be a reflection of our own automation. We struggle to express some form of release whilst unaware of the binds that biologically hold us back.

The consensus reality that is forming appears to point increasingly at the limitation of the human biological 'weak body.' In this, we must be wary of the mathematization of reality, where the quantitative replaces the qualitative as the measurement of human life. It is the quality of immersion, interaction, and participatory engagement that enhances the quality of human life and not detracts from it. We must desist the rising urge to critique the human body as vulnerable and 'weak' just because the narratives from technological elites are championing a trans-human future. Speaking of such futures, inventor and futurist Ray Kurzweil predicts that in the 2030s human brains will be able to connect to the cloud and to use it just like we use cloud computing today. That is, we will be able to transfer emails and photos directly from the cloud to our brain as well as backing up our thoughts and memories. How will this futuristic scenario be possible? Kurzweil says that nanobots - tiny robots constructed from DNA strands – will be swimming around in our brains. And the result? According to Kurzweil, we are going to be funnier, sexier, and better at expressing our loving sentiments. Not only will being connected to the computing cloud make humans sexier and funnier, it will apparently take us closer to our gods says Kurzweil: 'So as we evolve, we become closer to God. Evolution is a spiritual process. There is beauty and love and creativity and intelligence in the world - it all comes from the neocortex. So we're going to expand the brain's neocortex and become more godlike.'[5] It's hard to argue with such a bargain – a few nanobots in our brain to become godlike? I can imagine a lot of people tempted to sign up for this. *Chapel Perilous* is getting forever closer.

Robosapiens

The 'Great Reset' that is being pushed onto the global stage is a technocratic wet dream that envisions a 'Fourth Industrial Revolution' that will transform the way humans live, work, identify, and relate to one another. It is an agenda that envisions the merging of physical, digital, and biological worlds. It is none other than an integrated and entangled tech-enabled ecosystem where the human body becomes the subject rather than the driver. As the saying goes - industrialization didn't turn us into machines and automation isn't going to turn us into automatons. However, it may not be so clear cut. Remaining *authentically human* will not be that simple. Especially as an algorithmic landscape will represent an ecosystem and infrastructure based upon techno-linguistic automatism. Again, citing Berardi: 'the techno-linguistic automaton results from the intersection between artificial intelligence and big data, and acts as a prescriptive generator of life forms.'[6] A 'generator of life forms' – is this amalgam of AI with a physical-digital-biological fusion going to become the new 'life form'? If we listen to some of the top techie spokespeople on this, then it certainly seems so. Already the tentacles of surveillance capitalism have infiltrated or gained 'incursion' into the interior processes of the human body. As Professor Zuboff writes:

> Surveillance capital wants more than my body's coordinates in time and space. Now it violates the inner sanctum as machines and their algorithms decide the meaning of my breath and my eyes, my jaw muscles, the hitch in my voice, and the exclamation points that I offered in my innocence and hope.[7]

The trend now is deep machine-learning to the point where machines will not only learn data – such as from the 'inner sanctum' of the human body – to program themselves but will now use this information to program other machines also.

Cognitive computer scientists are attempting to re-capture the essence of human consciousness in the hope of back engineering this complexity into machine code. It may not actually be the sentient robots we need to worry about; it is the mindless ones we need to be cautious of. One of the methods used in training such robots is, in the words of their trainers, to provide them with enough 'intrinsic motivation.'[i] Not only will this help the robots to learn their environments, it is also hoped that it will foster attention in them to acquire sufficient situational awareness. Programmers are also talking about imbuing technologies and AI systems with values, ethics, and qualities that mark us out as human beings. However, humans are naturally vulnerable; it is part of our organic make-up. Whatever we 'create' may inherit those vulnerabilities.

Our very incompleteness is what gives us room to grow. As the Indian philosopher Sri Aurobindo repeatedly stated, the human is unfinished – evolution is not yet finished with us. Why the rush to trade the vehicle now? We still have the necessity to evolve and mature as a species; and we should not allow the world of transhumanism to deny us this great privilege. It would be a great waste, in this author's opinion, if people began to disappear behind their transhuman substitutes. If anything, we now need to become *more than human* yet within our biological humanity.

While the narratives are establishing an adapted language for a new coded environment – a language of humanity reduced to biological 'weak bodies' in the digital ecosystem – the focus is being taken away from the real centre.

---

i   For some discussion on this, see - https://futurism.com/what-will-the-rise-of-conscious-machines-mean-for-human-beings/

That is, ourselves. The trick of evolving within the landscape of the 'unreal machine' is by becoming more human, the very antithesis of the transhuman agenda. We would do well to remember that whilst technological tools can help us realize our dreams, they can also entrap us in theirs. Algorithms, smart machines, intelligent infrastructures, automated processes: these are all now becoming central to how we live our lives. The foreground of human civilization is increasingly being run, and ruled, from the background (and the background buzz). Such technologies should compel us to acknowledge our inherent human qualities and to uplift them, and not to turn us into a 'techno-compatible' species that devolves its humanity – the *Robosapien*.

The regime of biopower may result in turning the 'bio' against pure biology and morphing it into the 'new reign' of physical-digital-bio where the hybrid rules and life is mediated through code. One of the definitions of automation is 'a machine which performs a range of functions according to a predetermined set of coded instructions.' While we are experiencing the upsurge of a coded environment, with its techno-linguistic automaton, we may be witnessing the forced birth of a new order of 'neuro-techno totalitarianism' arising, to which I shall now address.

THIRTEEN

Neuro-Techno Totalitarianism

'We are now dealing with the two major forces of social consciousness and techno-evolution, and their merging.'

Franco 'Bifo' Berardi

It seems that the world, and those of us within it, are experiencing the merging of forces that were hitherto part of distinct realms. In the case of Franco Berardi, he considers this as principally the merging of human/social consciousness and techno-evolution. As discussed previously on the theme of biopower, the rise of modernity was mapped through the disciplining of the physical 'subject body.' That is, social and cultural institutions were developed to subdue and ultimately exert control and external 'expert' knowledge over the body. The human body, as a site of target, was relatively easy to identity and monitor. Now, however, we are entering a different realm where mind-consciousness-psyche - the intangible realm of *nous* - is the new digital-mental 'body' that is the site of target. Berardi recognizes this by saying that: 'Not the body but the soul becomes the subject of techno-social domination.'[1] And this, says Berardi, may likely lead to a new 'schizoidism' arising from this digital-mental body as human consciousness becomes confused by an exterior world at odds with its internal image, orientation, and equilibrium.

In these years, and the years ahead, humanity will be compelled to evolve/adapt to a different frequency range as the biological-digital landscape is manoeuvred into a new ecosystem of meaning. It will also be a novel realm where consciousness, digital-information, and augmented environments develop into an interacting network of symbols, signs, and significance. The social sphere is rapidly merging with the infosphere to form a new mutation – a new 'body.' This forms part of the emerging new consensus reality that this book discusses. And within this mutation, humanity will need to recalibrate what the 'social' means. The earlier notions of a communal social body, with recognizable cognitive and geographical form, has now shape-shifted into an architecture of surveillance, digital-tech networks, and monitored mobilities. The present is no longer linear. The future from here is not a straight line.

The global psycho-power agendas now arising to steer the 'Fourth Industrial Revolution' are intent on eradicating existing geographical categories and definitions. These players are promoting an architecture of overarching connectivity that meshes fleshy bodies, physical-digital infrastructures, and automated algorithms with coerced thinking patterns and promoted concepts – and all amid a rising degree of conscious awareness. The planet that we have known for so long as a fixed territory is morphing into a bio-digital-info super-organism. The question that needs to be asked is: how will this impact and influence not only human identity but human freedom and sovereignty? If the global players directing the political-financial-technological transition get their way, we may soon find ourselves belonging more to an 'unreal digital-physical machine' of programmed and automated codes of algorithmic conduct than a human-centric habitat.

This mutation of the global-urban environment into 'technological-complexes' is occurring at a pace more rapid than any previous social-cultural transition. It is changing faster than human cultural habits and social conditionings are accustomed to; and for many people, it is stressing them to the max. It may also be a case of more information but less meaning; and more stimuli but less genuine pleasure. Through this rapidly unfolding transition people from all backgrounds are being driven to renegotiate relations of meaning as a reprogramming and reorganization of human life comes into effect.

There is no doubt that a worldwide transformation is currently in process that will affect the future of human civilization upon this planet. This transformation (or mutation) will affect our individual and collective sense of perception and how we formulate and understand reality. It is critical that people do not enter this transformation without a minimum of awareness. We need to know, and accept, that *something* is coming, regardless of the final form it will take. This transmutation, or metamorphosis, must be recognized and explored in order for us to understand the experience of the world we are moving into. In the perspective of Franco Berardi, we have entered into a *technomaya* where we are forced to undergo a changed set of experiential relations with the world: 'We live in the multilayered dimension of technomaya...a spell that envelops the psychosphere.'[2] We need to confront the fact that our experiences of the world are going to be increasingly altered by technology as new forms of regulation, surveillance, and psycho-power emerge. What will eventually develop from this fluid mix of relations, networks, agendas, and population programming is still to be seen. However, Franco Berardi believes that the current global shifts in power relations, aligned with increasing forms of digital management, may very well result in the creation of a kind of 'techno-totalitarianism.' Let this be examined.

Techno-Totalitarianism

Humanity's past is littered with revolutions of one kind or another, whether social, political, or technological. There are times when an accumulation of disruption leads to a revolution of liberation; other times when it leads instead into a further consolidation of power. And in highly complex societies, power becomes increasingly intangible, and finally immaterial. The extreme of this is likely to be an automated form of incorporeal power wielded by governed systems that are non-visible and untouchable. As already noted, relations of power and authority are today pervasive throughout the many and various societies and cultures. The new reign of biopower and psycho-power lend themselves to a range of surveillant systems that combine traceability with predictability, determinism, and control. The increase in tracking and databasing human behaviour further allows technological systems to program and assess peoples' predictability. This very act of techno-surveillance reduces human behaviour into more predictability and certainty. This has already begun with the establishment of surveillance capitalism, which Professor Zuboff has stated signals 'the transformation of the market into a project of total certainty.'[3]

Once this happens, pre-emptive action becomes a standardized tool within the repertoire of power relations (as shown in Philip K. Dick's *Minority Report* story). Berardi sees this as becoming a form of techno-totalitarianism in the making 'as a process of standardization of cognition, perception, and behaviour based on the inscription of techno-linguistic automatisms in human communication, and therefore in the connective mind.'[4] This form of techno-totalitarianism, says Berardi, results from three consecutive steps that he describes as comprising i) the permanent connective wiring of interactions between humans; ii) the replacement of living experience; and iii) the insertion of techno-devices and enhancement of neural programming.

The first step - the permanent connective wiring of interactions between humans – Berardi refers to as a process of *cellularization*. This process he describes as the 'perfect carrier' of the socio-cognitive mutation. The mobile/

cellular phone, in particular, has created an infrastructure of global interconnection and opens the way to what Berardi sees as the 'ultimate deterritorialization' and ubiquity of information. He sees it as leading to the 'collectivization of personal lives' whereby individualism is subsumed into a form of commercial singularity. *Cellularization* also sets up a techno-linguistic system of exchange whereby people become less independent actors of their own behaviour and more controlled by the new techno-linguistic parameters. Social communication thus becomes subsumed into the 'electronic swarm,' as Berardi puts it. Language becomes more a form spoken by the technological system rather than technology being a subject of language.

The second step - the replacement of living experience – is similar to what has been described in terms of hyperreality and the notion of simulation (in Part One). It regards the replacement of current lived experience with the simulations of standardized and automated stimulus. This can also be seen occurring through the advancement of automations, augmented-reality, and the sense of the void and nihilism (see next chapter). There is a gradual acceptance of the 'replacement' of the lived experience. Experience is more than an event; it is a sensual encounter and the independent responses taken away from those encounters. If this process is somehow standardized, or customized-controlled, then we can see how Berardi views this as an act of techno-totalitarianism.

The third step - the insertion of techno-devices and enhancement of neural programming – moves away from the cognitive-psychological focus of the previous two steps and enters the terrain of hardware. It refers to the manipulation of neural systems through devices, prostheses, modifiers, and enhancers. Neural manipulation through biological, chemical, or technological intervention is already a growing area for exploration and experimentation. Several well-funded neurotechnology companies are already developing implantable brain-machine interfaces (BMIs); most notably is the Neuralink Corporation that was co-founded by tech-entrepreneur Elon Musk in 2016. Such explorations suggest acting upon brain neuroplasticity to create and reshape neuro-synaptic pathways. It opens the way for a huge intervention from biocapitalism - as well as authoritarian bodies – to enact psycho-sabotage or subversion through neuro-dominance. It is a dangerous terrain indeed, and the genii is already out of the bottle on this one.

Berardi asks whether it is possible, or even advisable, to resist this techno-mutation. He concludes that resistance may not be possible because technological innovation invariably reshapes the social environment. To resist would be to place the person first on the margins of their social milieu, and eventually outside forever (if this were possible). A person, and their family lineage, would effectively cease to have access to a world within the physical-digitally managed systems. The matrix of techno-totalitarianism would erase their data completely or absorb them utterly. The result could worryingly give rise to a *Neuro-Techno Totalitarianism* complex. Historically, the western world experienced an early version of such a system in the mid-twentieth century with the rise of Nazism.

The philosopher Karl Jaspers wrote that the fundamental feature of Nazism is techno-totalitarianism and that this may re-emerge through a further deployment and development of technology. Similarly, the philosopher Gunther Anders wrote:

> Doubtless, when one day our children or grandchildren, proud of their perfect 'co-mechanization', look down from the great heights of their thousand year Reich at yesterday's empire, at the co-called 'third' Reich, it will seem to them merely a minor, provincial experiment.[5]

Anders recognized the central feature of Nazism as being

automated inhumanity; and considered Nazism as the anticipation of the 'Reich to come.' He readily understood that the experimentation with technology as 'automated inhumanity' was not yet at an end. As Anders went on to note: 'Since Auschwitz, the machine of extermination has undergone a process of automation, and extermination has turned into an institutionalized task.'[6] Berardi, too, questions whether the rapid advancement of technology has led to the world falling away from our grasp, both physically and psychologically. He asks whether the world now emerging has become, or will become, 'too much' for us. Perhaps, our minds are already being rewired.

Neuro-Interventions

The environments around us are taking on a different rhythm; different landscapes will bring new sensory experiences and contexts for the human mind. How will we react? The accelerating development of autonomous technology and algorithmic systems will bring unprecedented change into our lives. First, however, they may bring disruptions and displacement into our lives and social relations. As a sentient, biological species, we must be prepared for both disruption and mutation – they come hand in hand. The entire nervous system of the human species will undergo a transformation throughout the years ahead as the techno-mutation shifts from a novelty into a normality. As a diverse, and now global, species we are set to undergo an evolutionary transmutation that will encompass the biological-cognitive-social-technological systems that frame our known reality. As I have emphasized throughout this book, humanity is witnessing a transition from one consensus reality into a new one. And it is my hope that this new reality can be more expansive, impressive, far-reaching, and assists in developing human perceptions and perspectives to grasp an understanding that is larger than ourselves. Yet, as I have pointed out in the previous chapters, there is also an organized, global program to manipulate and force this emerging 'reality narrative' into a scenario that supports a particular agenda of control and power. And the danger here is that this power agenda appears to be co-opting a path of transhumanism for its goals.

The entire history of life on this planet has been about mutation in all its forms. Yet now this process is speeding up as it is being both naturally and deliberately enhanced. The human being is going to be faced with a new realm of the senses:

> 'The process of transformation, which was the object of political imagination in modernity, is shifting to the conceptual and practical sphere of neuroplasticity. The mutation of the mind is underway. It is the consequence of a spasmodic attempt by individual minds to cope with a chaotic global infosphere, and to reframe the relation between the psychosphere and the infosphere, between cognition and stress, and between the brain and chaos.'[7]

The reality that is emerging is going to present to the modernizing world a modified psychological dimension. In the beginning, some may experience trauma or anxiety as different narratives are pushed into the world and propagandized. There will be a concerted effort, which has already begun, to get the majority of people believing in the main, dominant narrative – a narrative of digital acceleration and increased technologized social control. It is not only an external program but, as discussed, a form of psycho-power that aims to persuade and manage how people think. That is, not only a potential path of techno-totalitarianism but of a *neuro-techno totalitarianism*.

The human mind, well-known for its neuroplasticity, will be adapting to an expanding physical-digital ecosystem of shifted relations and networks. For some, this will subject the neural system to a sense of overload and cause discomfort. The development and increasing dominance of a 'smart' technological infrastructure will affect our social links and alliances. The whole human nervous system will be impacted from these changes, not only the mind. Those who support and are presenting the dominant narrative may use this as a push for transhumanism, calling it a necessary step forward in humanity's evolutionary biological mutation. Such a physical mutation will inevitably cause a cognitive one too. And yet most people are already subjected to a relentless and ongoing controlled cognitive mutation through the manipulated mainstream media with its propaganda and propagation of authoritative narratives. Over the years, humanity has been increasingly desensitized to the violence and absurdity of the world. The modern world has constructed its own bubble that anesthetizes and creates apathy and indifference to the manipulated and stage-managed events that have driven the world in its current direction. The social mind has been struggling against its own lobotomy. People have been programmed into a mode of competition and 'survival of the fittest' and conditioned to be dismissive of alternative ideas that go against the mainstream status quo. In this, we are being prepared to mimic the automation of the coming machinic assemblage of *neuro-techno totalitarianism*. As Berardi notes: 'The connective energies of the new generation have been recombined by the techno-financial automaton, and reduced to a condition of precariousness. Aggressive belonging is their only form of cohesion.'[8] And yet, at the same time, and within the very same processes, there is simultaneously the potential for neuro-emancipation and conscious evolution. The 'psychospiritual nature' of humanity can be activated and developed. 'Aggressive belonging' need not be the 'only form of cohesion.' The human vision and imagination can become a conscious pathway to a different future. But first, we need to face the spectre of nihilism and its cult of the irrational.

FOURTEEN

The New Nihilism
- a cult of the irrational?

'That there is no truth; that there is no absolute state of affairs - no "thing-in-itself." This alone is Nihilism, and of the most extreme kind.'

Friedrich Nietzsche

'There is no truth; there is no meaning; but we can create a bridge beyond the abyss of the non-existence of truth.'

Franco 'Bifo' Berardi

There is the potential, if not corrected, that the new 'mutation' - the social body - is rootless, and discontinuous with a past that has been deliberately dismantled and re-arranged through a newer model of consensus reality. People may be too eager and ready for a new 'revelation' to be given to them in replacement to a shattered and demolished prior reality worldview. This is nothing other than creating a collective 'mass minded' person rather than the unique individual of self-sovereignty. If nothing is done to halt the plays of psycho-power in operation, future humans may be confronted with a 'reduced' model of the homo sapiens, now referred to as the *Robosapien* – a being that is not inhuman but a-human. This is a human being that is not fully rooted in themselves. That is, their sense of a 'Self' is a shifting personality that roams according to external circumstances rather than grounded – rooted – with an anchoring of inner gravity. This rootlessness is the grounds for feelings of meaningless and insignificance in life. The danger is that if there is an escalation in the extremes of external power alongside an increasing sense of internal powerlessness, then the result may be a rising incoherence that paralyzes people into passivity.

As noted in the opening citations of this chapter, the question of nihilism is deeply rooted to the question, or notion, of truth – of what *is truth*? The most extreme kind of nihilism, according to Nietzsche, is that in the end, when all the layers are stripped away, there is no 'thing-in-itself.' The 'truths' of our present age are only relative truths and are presented either in the 'academic sciences' that are continually in debate, or argument, over such truths – or they are the 'truths' propagated to the masses through the mainstream media. The current age has no *assembly of knowledge* or authority of truth. Everything is comparative, relative, and in flux. Truth is nowadays that which is according to each observer, based on a mixture of assumptions and opinions. The concept of 'Truth' is itself an object of scientific analysis; it is poked and prodded, defined, and redefined and reinterpreted. Old forms are being emptied and given a new content relative to the time and narrative that is wished to be conveyed. The present age is full of prefixes of truth – post-truth, fake-truth, old-paradigm-truth, and the rest. Truth can no longer stand alone. Or so it seems.

Nietzsche noted that, 'Of all that which was formerly held to be true, not one word is to be credited. Everything which was formerly disdained as unholy, forbidden, contemptible, and fatal - all these flowers now bloom on the most charming paths of truth.'[1] The question over truth is also a question of value. And as Nietzsche understood, the issue was that the highest values are in the process of losing, or have already lost, their value. Then where is the goal – the significance? Nietzsche concluded by saying that there is no answer to the question: 'Why?' Why should anyone do anything in a world that is less and less clear to us, and increasingly seeming absurd? This may be the conundrum – the existential crisis – of the post-2020 world.

The play of psycho-power in the world is resulting in greater forms of authoritarian absurdity being pressed upon the minds of the people. This is heightened by the folly of the mainstream media and the entertainment industry. It now appears, for all intents and purposes, that the modern era has transitioned into the Age of Absurdity. It is an age of absurdism as recognized by its high degree of jargon, jingles, and memes. It has taken the role of critical perception and placed it into acronyms and popularist memes. To transcend the absurdity of the modern world is almost the same question as how to transcend the perceptual limits of the world. A certain form of inner recognition is required for both. In a world where forms of absurdism reign, meaning, significance, and purpose all lose out. It is an arena where things fall apart because they no longer have any centre to hold them together. And yet, in some absurd way, a form of 'mainstream daily life' continues. Perhaps it is this which characterizes the life of the Robosapien? There is no sense of a 'normal' age in which we live, despite the exaggerated claims to want to strive or return to a normality - was there ever a normality? How too can there be a claim to wish to create a 'new normality' when this term itself is a false construction? This is part of the absurdism of our times and is a profound symptom of humanity's inner state and psyche, and of the balance within the self. It is like an affirmation of the Abyss, an attraction to the Void, as Baudrillard would say.

Humanity is being thrust now into a mode of reorientation; of trying to navigate the landscape of the absurd. It is 'a landscape in which there is neither up nor down, right nor wrong, true nor false, because there is no longer any commonly accepted point of orientation.'[2] There seems to be less and less of a trail, a marked path, or any sense of a guiding Ariadne's thread through the labyrinth. People are being forced to adopt the uncertainty almost unknowingly, yet willingly. An empty hole of significance is not the heart but the symptom of these times. And it is because of this that humanity is circling very close to an existential whirlpool. Within an existential crisis, absurdism becomes an *internal* question as much as an external one. The individual comes face-to-face with their own incoherency.

What are the Questions?

The phenomenon of nihilism can be recognized as a broader movement, or collective state, in which the psycho-mental state of existentialism affects humanity. This state of affairs shows that everything has become questionable. Fewer people are asking the ultimate questions; and even fewer are seeking the answers. An aura of scepticism and disbelief has crept into the social fabric. The external institutions of control are attempting to confuse coercion by gradually replacing it by internal self-persuasion. Under these terms, the greater questions that come from the self are either blocked or eliminated. Not having a basis or grounding of truth within the individual only serves to further self-interest and desires for material gain. These are the signs of a reality increasingly founded on untruths and unknowns. The unfolding consensus reality is based on a great unknowability and their attendant narratives. In the words of Seraphim Rose:

> ...Nihilism has become, in our time, so widespread and pervasive, has entered so thoroughly and so deeply into the minds and hearts of all men living today, that there is no longer any "front" on which it may be fought; and those who think they are fighting it are most often using its own weapons, which they in effect turn against themselves.[3]

A sense of truth – especially inner truths – is a grounding energy. It helps to moor us to a state of stability and equilibrium. When aspects of reality no longer have any relation to truths, there is a loss of anchoring. Within this fluidity – this void – elements of the 'absurd' are free to enter. Narratives of 'everything is relative' supports the priority of short-term sensations and distractions over genuine, long-term inner nourishment. In other words, it is a fast-food world of temporary satisfactions without fundamental stability. In such an environment, there is a lack of authenticity. The authentic and genuine gets replaced by the reproduction (as Walter Benjamin knew very well).[i]

Without this grounding of the genuine and authentic, an inner disquiet creeps in. This disquiet is seen by the plethora of distractions that rise up to meet this need, which are more often than not played out by the 'new spiritualities' of the age - a time for gurus, magicians, and phony prophets. Yet these are the retreats from the encroaching malaise of restlessness and meaninglessness. They represent the existential crisis of 'falling away from one's being' - a de-centeredness that creates disorientation. What I am pointing to here is not the political form of Nihilism but a psychological one. Perhaps it may be better served by calling it 'Post-Truth Nihilism.' It is a psychosphere – a sense of reality – where denial and disbelief play at being the core aspects around a realm of insincerity and fakery. Out of this is where arises the 'world of the absurd' that feeds into the new replacement consensus reality. It is a realm where irrationality becomes a new form of narrative.

The Cult of Irrationality

This 'New Nihilism' – or the cult of irrationality - represents

---

i   See Walter Benjamin's essay "The Work of Art in the Age of Mechanical Reproduction" (1935)

a general dissatisfaction with the way things are. It does not wish for a return to the old ways, despite its pretence and protestations. It wants a new replacement authority. Perhaps one that will be used to support a new Reset? Yet in the extreme of such dismantling, where can people go to find themselves – the root of themselves?

In the past, regimes (such as Fascism and National Socialism) have exploited this sense of restlessness to feed into their own purposes and eventual authoritarianism. This is because, in order to build a new Order, a new form of world structure, it is necessary first to dismantle the old narratives that held the old order together. In many cases, it is regarded as preferable to crush the old systems and ways of thinking so that their remnants do not try to rise up to confront the new programming. This was seen with the National Socialism of the Nazis - it wasn't only a new physical order that they were creating but also, just as importantly, a psychological one. The new replacement structure must clear a fresh path to pave the way for declaring a new security state. In our times, this includes a new world order of biosecurity.

It can clearly be seen how new forms of social-political organization are being established upon the physical-digital platforms of a technological era. This represents an era of nihilism, where *technique* and precision are paramount, and which display an evident insensitivity toward the individual and the very 'being' of humanity. Such 'Nihilist organization' represents 'the total transformation of the earth and society by machines...and the inhuman philosophy of "human engineering" that accompanies them.'[4] The overt structure of nihilist societies is that the smaller, relative truths are co-opted in serving the dominant narratives of power. This is because, if there are no recognized great truths then secular power has no limits except those that are imposed by human authority. The trick here is passing off such a state of absurdism as the new realism. Yet this façade actually not only creates a state of deep existential crisis within humanity but also establishes the most efficient prison possible for it will be unperceived by the senses until a time when there will be no way of getting away from it and nowhere to go.

The breakdown and dismantling of the older structures and systems, and the replacement with 'new normal' systems of the 'Great Reset' is the most ambitious and audacious reprogramming and reorganization of human life ever attempted thus far in the known history of humanity. It represents nothing less than the transformation of humankind into a new organization of the species body. This 'Great Reset' form of organization is nihilistic in its extreme, lacking any empathy or recognition of core human values. It is a blatant move towards standardization, automation, and dehumanization. It is the reduction of the individual to the automaton of the *Robosapien* where the biological community is replaced by the automaton collective. And the automaton collective is one that is both fuelled and ruled by data.

The individual sense of self is being broken down and fragmented into bits of digital data for the machine of our human societies. As philosopher Byung-Chul Han says: 'Dataism is nihilism. It gives up on any and all meaning. Data and numbers are not narrative; they are additive. Meaning, on the other hand, is based on narration. Data simply fills up the senseless void.'[5] With enough data, the numbers will create their own definition of the world. And this world picture may very likely end up constructing the consensus reality narrative that gets pushed onto the human collective and into our nervous-system senses. This is the 'neuro-techno totalitarianism' spoken of in the previous chapter.

We must be wary of the global technosphere becoming monopolized by the monolithic tech giants that feed into a transnational Leviathan superstructure. It could be a superstructure run on AI data that replaces the act of human thinking with an automated simulation of cognition. These processes are already managing our infrastructures and forms of communication and connectivity. Authenticity is being replaced by replication. Perhaps humanity is entering a period of impotence that follows on from the accomplishment of absurdity into abstraction. And in its wake, 'computation has taken the place of all-encompassing nature, and the rules of the automaton seem to be as inescapable as natural laws.'[6] As the philosopher Franco Berardi notes, a 'blackout on sensibility' has occurred in the world - a blackout on human good reason and common sense. The end of one history has taken place almost imperceptible to most people, and an abyss has opened up to allow top-down forces that seem intent on sabotaging our capacity to conceptualize a new human vision: 'Our impotence to imagine, to criticize and to choose is deepening as our technological potency, and the growing automation of technological procedures, are expanding.'[7] Yet as Berardi's citation to this chapter states, even in these times of inauthenticity and untruths, we can create a bridge beyond this abyss.

 Nietzsche too saw this way out, this crack of opportunity within the encroaching machine of modern life. He said that under certain circumstances, '*Nihilism* might be the sign of a process of incisive and most essential growth, and of mankind's transit into completely new conditions of existence. *This is what I have understood.*'[8] There is perhaps a path now opening to seek transcendence to a new understanding within the unfolding consensus reality. And maybe, just maybe, humanity can turn to a form of *heretical consciousness*. The rise of the heretics could be upon the horizon.

FIFTEEN

Rise of the Heretics

'...the physical survival of the human race depends on a radical change of the human heart.'

Erich Fromm

'If humanity is to survive, a radical transformation of human nature is indispensable.'

Sri Aurobindo

As has been shown throughout this book, the rising technological-surveillance landscape is massively amplifying the societal impulse to conform. People are being 'data-fied' and treated more as 'massified objects' rather than as individuals. The reign of biopower is simultaneously moving in around us externally as well as entering into our bodies and, through strategies of psycho-power, into our minds. These forces of conformity are congealing into the new consensus reality that will compel people to increasingly accept the dominant narratives. That is, to think less critically for themselves and to be more passive in accepting what 'truths' and information (and/or propaganda) is provided for them. This consensus reality is suppressing *idiotisms*.

The 'real idiot' is the heretic, as such a figure represents the person of resistance against consensus and controlled thinking. The 'real idiot' preserves the advantage and enchantment of the outsider. And, by a pleasing coincidence, the Arabic word for 'Saint' (*wali*) has the same numerical equivalent as the word for 'Idiot' (*balid*). So, perhaps there is a double motive here for encouraging and developing what I refer to as *heretical consciousness*? And what is this consciousness? It is a form of perspective/perception that is vertical rather than horizontal. It does not operate within the horizontality of the system but pushes vertically upwards in order to gain a perspective 'from higher up' over and above the system. Further, etymologically, *heresy* means 'choice,' and a heretic is one who demands free choice, to deviate from consensus thinking, and against the power of the dominant narrative. That is, to seek for a transcendent perception within the consensus reality is the mark of *heretical consciousness*.

Such an 'idiot' or heretical consciousness does not readily accept the assumptions that pertain to group/collective thinking. Consensus thinking aims to develop a stable community, as in social management. And such a management generally requires that people do not question or critically engage with its dominant assumptions. And yet, somewhat ironically, the majority of people seek group-association and a 'community of belonging.' This fits in very well with the cultivation of an obedience to authority as, in return, the obedient are given security, safety, and belonging – as discussed in Chapter Ten. As mentioned previously, people have become automatons who live under the illusion of being self-willing individuals. In general, life within modern industrialized societies has been based upon living within dependency-orientated cultures. Within this psychological framework, social members tend to be more preoccupied with seeking out comfort and reassurance. Not necessarily because they need it but rather because they are used to it. In other words, people have a tendency to steer towards retaining and reinforcing their comfort zones. And the more this is encouraged by the society/culture, the more it is reinforced by the individual, as if within a negative feedback loop.

In order to break from these bonds that prevent further individual development it is necessary to inculcate a heretical consciousness by first thinking differently; that is, by perceiving the consensus narratives from an off-centre perspective. Heretical thinking is about perceiving the possibilities beyond one's present state. By continuing to think within the current framework, a person can only advance their perspectives within that framework. As has been emphasized throughout this book, there is an aim to reprogram human life through presenting a new consensus reality. Yet a reprogramming does not provide the flexibility for a heretical consciousness for it is still a program. Dominant narratives serve to replace one program with another, yet still within the dominant framework. Genuine autonomy of perceptive insight is not what the dominant consensus seeks. The heretical idiot plays the game by knowing it is a game. But it is the social idiot who is played by the game without awareness of this.

At the end of the previous chapter, it was noted that Nietzsche saw within nihilism the possibility that it may also provide the means for humanity to 'transit into completely new conditions of existence.' What are these conditions, we may wonder? It is my perspective that Nietzsche recognized the powerful flow of vital forces within life. In the end, it could be said that Nietzsche himself fell prey to these vital forces. And yet Nietzsche lamented the loss of transcendental forces operating within human life. For this reason, he felt compelled to assert the need for people to strengthen their 'will to power.' This is not the external form of physical power but rather the strength of the individual self – to live through the force of one's own inherent will and intention. Such forces often operate also through physical, emotional, and power structures. They are those forces that one often calls 'magnetic.' They attract as much as they repel. They animate as much as they destroy. These are the forces that can be 'hijacked' to propel materialism and support externalized power structures. These are the energies that offer the whirlwind of modern life. And yet, as Berardi remarks, it is 'Only inside the whirlwind will the clue to the new rhythm be found.'[1] Only from within the maelstrom of life itself will any answers be found. They will not be found by seeking them in caves, retreats, or on mountain tops. And yet, the passionate centre of life is where the whirlwind blows strongest. The chains of vital energies that tie us into systems of control and power operate through such vitalism. People are distracted and disempowered through their bodily restrictions; hence, the targeting of biopower and biosecurity upon the human body. The transhumanist agenda seeks to gradually divest the human body of its principal motive force. The human body is being targeted for hybridization and recombination as a means of restraining the engine of human force. And yet authentic human power functions through psychic power (which also includes the authentic human heart). Also, importantly, the vital powers can be manipulated to encourage the external mode of possession and 'having,' while the psychic power supports and nourishes the inner mode of self-possession and 'being.' And it will be the true heretics, with heretical consciousness, who can make this distinction from living in a 'having' mode to a 'being' mode.

    The social psychologist Erich Fromm (discussed in Chapter Ten) recognized that the more a person *has*, the less they are attracted to making active and constructive efforts. He saw a clear connection between the relationship to external objects and desires, and inner laziness. And it was this inner laziness that would ultimately form a vicious circle, reinforcing the need to stay in the comfort zone of 'having' and relying upon external dependencies. He stated that,

> ...modern man *has* many things and uses many things, but he *is* very little. His feelings and thinking processes are atrophied like unused muscles. He is afraid of any crucial social change because any disturbance in the social balance to him spells chaos or death - if not physical death, the death of his identity.[2]

And yet, ironically, the rise of biopower and a controlled consensus reality is the very thing that will contribute to the accelerated demise of the individual identity as it becomes data-fied and lodged as a digital identity. Perhaps the only real way to counteract this influence is to strengthen the reverse of this – one's *inner identity*. That is, the 'being' of the individual.

To Be or Not To Be – the heretical question

There is the continual, and rising, danger here of external expressions of 'well-being' becoming co-opted by the consensus system to serve as developing the inner chains within us. What is needed is not an external, systemic shift but a psychological one. As philosopher Sri Aurobindo put it: 'Without an inner change man can no longer cope with the gigantic development of the outer life.'[3] The evolution of human civilization does not stem from a structural change, a shift in its institutions and systems, but from a psychological change within the human being. In other words, the future will come about according to human consciousness and not the other way around. Whereas Aurobindo recognized this as being an intuitive, gnostic consciousness, I refer to it in the current context as a heretical consciousness for it transcends, and is opposing, the dominant consensus narrative group-consciousness.

Such periods of history as humanity is presently experiencing are rooted more in the psychological evolution of humankind than any external classifications. The globalist identification is one of a 'Fourth Industrial Revolution' as they see the future in terms of a technological-based capitalism. The globalist-influenced consensus reality does not recognize the *psychological beingness* of the individual. And yet, any authentic future for the human species can *only* be based on the very nature of this *beingness*. Of course, the central question remains: how can such a large-scale shift toward *beingness* be made possible in our present way of life and attitude?

Erich Fromm suggests the following conditions that would be necessary to stimulate such a fundamental shift in human nature:

i) We are suffering and are aware that we are.
ii) We recognize the origin of our ill-being.
iii) We recognize that there is a way of overcoming our ill-being.
iv) We accept that in order to overcome our ill-being we must follow certain norms for living and change our present practice of life.[4]

These may appear to be simplistic conditions, yet clear recognition of the human predicament is paramount. Fromm initially calls on a need to 'change our present practice of life,' which, on first reading, sounds naïve. Yet Fromm was not blind to the difficulties of the situation and the obstructions people would likely place as excuses to refrain from such a course of action. He noted that: 'yet another explanation for the deadening of our survival instinct is that the changes in living that would be required are so drastic that people prefer the future catastrophe to the sacrifice they would have to make now.'[5]

Fromm was insistent that *insight separated from practice remains ineffective*. That is, if people don't put into action the thoughts and ideas they have, then nothing will be attained. The two must correspond and be in relation to form the third force of actualization – thought (passive) with action (active) forms a manifested result (integral whole). The problem that faces people today is that their passage to radical, yet necessary, social change lies blocked by a pervasive infrastructure of authoritarian control dictated by advanced forms of technological surveillance and data-management. The path to a *Being* society is obstructed by the rapid rise of a modern political establishment increasingly close to a technocracy.

Still, the power of the incumbent system did not stop Fromm, in his time, from discussing the need for a new society to be formed that would itself encourage the emergence of the 'heretical' human being. He outlined the following traits as being the qualities of this new human:

- A willingness to give up forms of 'having' in order to truly 'be.'

- A sense of identity, security, and confidence based on one's self – what one 'is' – and with a need for relation with the world around instead of a desire to possess and control the world around oneself.

- An acceptance of the fact that nobody and nothing outside of oneself can give meaning to life – yet this independence in turn creates a full responsibility to care and share with others.

- Being fully present where one is.

- Joy and happiness come from giving and sharing rather than greed, hoarding, and exploitation.

- Love and respect for life in all its manifestations - in the recognition that things and power do not bring satisfaction and meaning but rather those things which are part of a living ecology.

- The need to reduce greed, hate, and delusions – to liberate oneself from these traps.

- To live in a state where illusions have no power over oneself – no need to worship external idols.

- Developing a heightened capacity for love, compassion, and understanding – without falling into sentimentalized emotions.

- Letting go of one's narcissism and ego-centric ideals – to recognize one's fallibility as a human being.

- Making the full growth of oneself and of one's fellow beings as the supreme goal of living – and knowing that to reach this goal requires discipline and respect.

- To develop one's imagination not as an escape from circumstances but as a means to create a vision of the real possibilities inherent within humankind.

- To not deceive others as well as not allowing oneself to be deceived by others – better to be innocent than naïve.

- To get to know the full depth of oneself, including the darker, shadow side.

- To develop a sense of the interrelatedness of all life – and to give up on the idea of wishing to conquer, control, and manipulate the environment.

- To develop a sense and meaning of freedom that is not random but a real possibility, consciously directed and within a responsible framework that is free from greed and selfish desire.

- To recognize that decay and destructiveness are the consequences that come from anti-growth and artificial forms of control.

- To recognize that perfection can be an ambition based in greed, and to allow a state of beingness that has imperfections.

- To accept that happiness is forever in the process of 'ever-growing aliveness' – and that living as fully as one can is a pleasant satisfaction as part of this journey.

These are high ideals indeed, yet not beyond the capacity of the human being. Until now, many instances of human freedom have, in the words of Fromm, been more successful in establishing the freedom of *whim* rather than the freedom of *will*. That is, where 'whim' responds to the question of 'why not?' - implying that a person does something simply because there is no reason for not doing it. Yet the active aspect of 'will' is a constructive response to the need for doing something. Reasons must have meaning, and through exercising authentic human will, we give ourselves meaning. Through human will, the individual can exercise concentration, focus, and directed intention. The individual can provide their activities with conscious attention and give force to their actions. This in turn helps each person to be centred, grounded, and balanced.

However, a person cannot be a force for change in their lives if they remain chained to the conditioned perceptions that propagate the mainstream consensus narrative. In this light, the heretic is one who perceives through the lens of magical thinking.

Magical Thinking

We already live in a world of magic and magical thinking, only that it has been passed off as part of the regular social programming. But 'magical thinking' is that which ascribes meaning and significance to signs, symbols, talismans; also, it seeks to find patterns and correspondences in seemingly non-related events. As discussed in Chapters Three and

Four, we live in a world of memes, celluloid signs, and hyperreality. Advertising logos work as magical symbols: we see a talismanic sigil, and immediately we associate a set of meanings and correspondences to it. Our minds start to cross-reference patterns of meaning, whether it be for fast-food or sportswear. Magical incantations have morphed into political speak of neurolinguistic programming language. Magical rituals have been transformed into huge stadiums full of participatory priests, priestesses, and applauding neophytes. A landscape of magical spells is continuously attempting to lure us into associated, programmed behaviours. The shift from an Enlightenment scientific-rational culture into a magical thinking one has already been achieved. Now the 'magical battle' is between casting a spell on humanity for a consensus reality, and simultaneously a contrary push away from the consensus experience and into the reality of individual experience.

Magical – that is, heretical – thinking from the individual is a perspective that seeks meaning and significance; it looks for patterns, relations, and correspondences rather than links. And importantly, authentic magical thinking and awareness is about recognizing that one is playing a game, and that there are different sets of rules to choose from, not only one. And that each individual can also create their own rules to play within the overall game. This path develops and accelerates human evolution, and evolutionary thinking, as it encourages new modes of experience, understanding, and perception. Where there is social conditioning, indoctrination, and a consensus programming there is a mechanical element involved. In present circumstances it can be said that this 'mechanical element' is not an accident for its presence drives out the factor of extradimensional reality perception which connects the higher functions of the mind with the higher reality. This 'higher reality' transcends the consensus reality programming and activates individual perceptual experiences that lie beyond the ken of the worldly mundane. The everyday world, with its reality programming, appeals to the deeper layers of the older evolutionary mind that include the reptilian complex (survival/reproduction) and the limbic 'mammalian' system (emotional) – both of which are highly responsive to external fear influences. Hence, the incoming consensus reality that is being pushed through the biopower agenda is operating through creating and propagating fear strategies (such as the virus-targeted biological 'weak body').

It is now necessary for human beings to activate their 'higher mind' thinking and to eliminate their dependency, or over-reliance, upon lower brain influences. Part of this is what I refer to as shifting into a heretical consciousness. It involves breaking the spell from fear-based programming and mass-orientated consensus reality narratives. It is a path of personal perceptual experience and, as Fromm states, depends on a radical change of the human heart. Likewise, Sri Aurobindo refers to this necessity by saying that a radical transformation of human nature is indispensable. This is the crossroads where humanity now finds itself at. This may also represent a crossroads where *reality splits*. That is, most people will unthinkingly follow the dominant, or herd, consensus reality whilst a minority – the heretics – will chose a reality where magical thinking operates, and human authenticity is more important than institutional inclusion. Almost as if sensing a parallel reality, those individuals of heretical consciousness will veer away from blindly adopting the consensus view and will choose instead to seek those sources that nourish the human interior life. They will make a conscious decision not to get pulled into the general 'gamified reality' and instead will reinforce their own perceptions and perspectives that provide greater meaning for them. Perhaps we have come to a time where a minor, yet still significant, number of human individuals have arrived where they are sufficiently prepared to uphold and sustain an alternative reality – that of the 'heretic,' for now.

The next decade will be a hugely important one for defining the future path that humanity will take. Within this decade, choices will be made that will either support and encourage the development of the human *being*; or, the transhumanist path of the 'weak body' will be sought that will take the majority of humanity along the route eerily close to neuro-techno totalitarianism (as discussed in Chapter Thirteen). The choice may be made for us, if individuals choose to do nothing.

The individual is now compelled to develop their senses, along with their good sense. Each person needs to be made aware of the choices that lie ahead of them, and of the possibilities, options, and opportunities they may face. And then to make decisions and act upon these accordingly. The decisions made by each individual will eventually inform the overall life experience – for better or for worse. Let us try to make each individual experience count.

AFTERWORD

You have never been amiss but merely only ever missed the point

and that be your own, you see?

Anon

The outer world seems to be pursuing a headlong rush into a hasty future. The external systems of management and control have made it clear that they are developing a different rhythm. It is a hurried rhythm that dances to the tune of technological time-beats and frantic identification with an environment that can be regarded as an 'artificial construct.' It has very little to do with the human 'self' and the *being* mode. Many people are now being forced to run fast just in order to remain in their spot. Yet this is not a human rhythm.

It seems that too many people spend too much effort trying to straighten out their lives while simultaneously missing the point of it. Like our canine friends, we are running in circles chasing our tails. There is an agenda, as this book has explained, to reprogram and replace a dominant consensus reality – and the human being is not at the heart of it. The reprogramming and reorganization of human life across various societies and cultures that is now underway is happening in a rush before too many people awaken to the situation and pull out their compliance. There are going to be many attempts to implement significant changes within the coming years. Before this happens, the heart of humanity needs to gather itself. People need to force a different rhythm – one that is more conducive to the human being. As it is said: that which is manifest in time is subject to the ravages of time. Perhaps it is now time to take 'time out' to a different mode in our lives.

Human life can be harsh and debilitating; and yet, there is a streak of coherence that connects us. There is not life and us; there is not planet and us; there is not universe and us. Everything is in relation. And the reorganization of human life trying to take dominance does not reflect this. But it is the time now for the human species to insist on these relational correspondences; upon the higher 'heretical' thinking that touches the multidimensional realm. Perhaps this is not what the majority of people are used to. Some may draw back, and retreat into the arms of a controlling external authority. Yet the true authentic authority lies deep within each individual. And life requires our conscious and willing participation.

It is necessary now to become *rooted* within ourselves. To gather our parts back together before they become scattered to the digital-identity wind. There is much going on in the world that seems like a pantomime. Many people are getting sucked into this 'phantom pantomime' more than they realize. We each need to find those sources that nourish us – that nourishes our lives – and bring them closer to us. In these current times especially, it will not help but hinder us if we become too entangled in these outer chains. As the world hurries headlong into its constructed story of a 'super convenient' controlled future, each individual needs to find the secure grounding within themselves. It is the human *being* that shall become the future – not our appliances.

Hijacking reality is about overtaking the natural *beingness* of the human state and charging ahead into an artificially dominant way of life. I have, in my own way, attempted to argue against this. Multiple layers of the Game are in play now. We can each choose the rules of our own gameplay – and enjoy playing the heretic.

January 2021

REFERENCES

Introduction

[1] Wilson, E.O. (2003). *The Future of Life*. London, Vintage, p28

Chapter One

[1] Baudrillard, J. (2008). *The Perfect Crime*. London, Verso, p1

[2] Baudrillard, J. (2008). *The Perfect Crime*. London, Verso, p53

[3] Baudrillard, J. (2008). *The Perfect Crime*. London, Verso, p100

[4] Han, B.-C. (2017). *Psycho-Politics: Neoliberalism and New Technologies of Power*. London, Verso.

[5] Berardi, F. (2019). *The Second Coming*. Cambridge, Polity Press, p90

[6] Berardi, F. (2019). *The Second Coming*. Cambridge, Polity Press, p2

Chapter Two

[1] Berardi, F. (2019). *The Second Coming*. Cambridge, Polity Press, p95-6

[2] Berardi, F. (2019). *The Second Coming*. Cambridge, Polity Press, p2

[3] Berardi, F. (2019). *The Second Coming*. Cambridge, Polity Press, p116

⁴ Cited in Han, B.-C. (2017). *Psycho-Politics: Neoliberalism and New Technologies of Power.* London, Verso, p67

⁵ Delsol, Chantal. (2003). *Icarus Fallen: The Search for Meaning in an Uncertain World.* Wilmington, DE: ISI Books, p214

⁶ Berardi, F. (2009). *The Soul at Work: From Alienation to Autonomy.* Los Angeles, CA, Semiotext(e), p200

⁷ Bauman, Zygmunt; Mauro, Ezio. 2016. *Babel.* Cambridge: Polity Press, p74-5

Chapter Three

¹ Berardi, F. (2019). *The Second Coming.* Cambridge, Polity Press, p125

² Cited in Levy, Paul. (2013). *Dispelling Wetiko: Breaking the Curse of Evil.* Berkeley, CA: North Atlantic Books, p192

³ Berardi, Franco. (2015). *AND: Phenomenology of the End.* South Pasadena, CA: Semiotext(e), p146

⁴ Berardi, Franco. (2015). *AND: Phenomenology of the End.* South Pasadena, CA: Semiotext(e), p220

⁵ Berardi, Franco. (2015). *AND: Phenomenology of the End.* South Pasadena, CA: Semiotext(e), p299

Chapter Four

¹ Han, B.-C. (2017). *Psycho-Politics: Neoliberalism and New Technologies of Power.* London, Verso, p12

² Han, B.-C. (2017). *Psycho-Politics: Neoliberalism and New Technologies of Power.* London, Verso, p9

³ Han, B.-C. (2017). *Psycho-Politics: Neoliberalism and New Technologies of Power.* London, Verso, p15

⁴ Floridi, Luciano. (2016). *The 4th Revolution: How the Infosphere is Reshaping Human Reality.* Oxford: Oxford University Press.

⁵ Floridi, Luciano. (2016). *The 4th Revolution: How the Infosphere is Reshaping Human Reality.* Oxford: Oxford University Press, p98

Chapter Six

¹ Vallee, J. (2008). *Revelations: Alien Contact & Human Deception.* San Antonio, TX, Anomalist Books.

² Vallee, J. (2008). *Dimensions: A Casebook of Alien Contact.* San Antonio, TX, Anomalist Books, p159

³ Vallee, J. (2008). *Dimensions: A Casebook of Alien Contact.* San Antonio, TX, Anomalist Books, p277

Chapter Nine

¹ Han, B.-C. (2017). *Psycho-Politics: Neoliberalism and New Technologies of Power.* London, Verso, p2

² Han, B.-C. (2017). *Psycho-Politics: Neoliberalism and New Technologies of Power.* London, Verso, p30

³ Berardi, F. (2019). *The Second Coming.* Cambridge, Polity Press, p11

⁴ Berardi, F. (2019). *The Second Coming.* Cambridge, Polity Press, p44-5

Chapter Ten

¹ Fromm, E. (1960). *The Fear of Freedom.* London, Routledge & Kegan Paul.

² Fromm, E. (1960). *The Fear of Freedom.* London, Routledge & Kegan Paul, p177

³ Fromm, E. (1993). *The Art of Being.* London, Constable, p7

⁴ Cited in Bauman, Zygmunt. (2006). *Liquid Fear.* Cambridge: Polity Press, p149

⁵ Cited in Zuboff, S. (2019). *The Age of Surveillance Capitalism: The Fight for a Human Future at the New Frontier of Power.* London, Profile Books, p355

⁶ Cited in Bauman, Zygmunt. (2006). *Liquid Fear.* Cambridge: Polity Press, p176

⁷ Bauman, Zygmunt; Lyon, David. (2013). *Liquid Surveillance.* Cambridge: Polity Press, p104

Chapter Eleven

¹ Lianos, Michalis, (2003) *'Social Control After Foucault',* Surveillance & Society 1(3): 412-430, p415

² Berardi, Franco. 2015. *AND: Phenomenology of the End.* South Pasadena, CA: Semiotext(e), p88

³ Online source - https://theintercept.com/2020/05/08/andrew-cuomo-eric-schmidt-coronavirus-tech-shock-doctrine/

⁴ ibid

⁵ ibid

⁶ Online source - https://www.bloomberg.com/news/articles/2020-05-01/the-office-you-left-is-not-going-to-be-the-office-you-return-to

⁷ Han, B.-C. (2017). *Psycho-Politics: Neoliberalism and New Technologies of Power.* London, Verso, p76

[8] Han, B.-C. (2017). *Psycho-Politics: Neoliberalism and New Technologies of Power.* London, Verso, p58

[9] Berardi, F. (2019). *The Second Coming.* Cambridge, Polity Press, p12

[10] Berardi, F. (2019). *The Second Coming.* Cambridge, Polity Press, p40

[11] Berardi, F. (2019). *The Second Coming.* Cambridge, Polity Press, p78

Chapter Twelve

[1] Berardi, F. (2019). *The Second Coming.* Cambridge, Polity Press, p41

[2] Berardi, F. (2019). *The Second Coming.* Cambridge, Polity Press, p20

[3] Harari, Yuval Noah. (2017). *Homo Deus - A Brief History of Tomorrow.* London: Vintage, p97.

[4] Berardi, F. (2019). *The Second Coming.* Cambridge, Polity Press, p77-8

[5] Miles, Kathleen, 'Ray Kurzweil: In The 2030s, Nanobots In Our Brains Will Make Us 'Godlike'', Huffington Post, 10th January 2015, http://www.huffingtonpost.com/entry/ray-kurzweil-nanobots-brain-godlike_us_560555a0e-4b0af3706dbe1e2

[6] Berardi, F. (2019). *The Second Coming.* Cambridge, Polity Press, p40

[7] Zuboff, S. (2019). *The Age of Surveillance Capitalism: The Fight for a Human Future at the New Frontier of Power.* London, Profile Books, p290

Chapter Thirteen

[1] Berardi, F. (2009). *The Soul at Work: From Alienation to Autonomy.* Los Angeles, CA, Semiotext(e), p200

[2] Berardi, Franco. (2015). *AND: Phenomenology of the End.* South Pasadena, CA: Semiotext(e), p299

[3] Zuboff, S. (2019). *The Age of Surveillance Capitalism: The Fight for a Human Future at the New Frontier of Power.* London, Profile Books, p20

[4] Berardi, Franco. (2015). *AND: Phenomenology of the End.* South Pasadena, CA: Semiotext(e), p311

[5] Cited in Berardi, F. (2019). *The Second Coming.* Cambridge, Polity Press, p36-7

[6] Cited in Berardi, F. (2019). *The Second Coming.* Cambridge, Polity Press, p38

[7] Berardi, Franco. (2015). *AND: Phenomenology of the End.* South Pasadena, CA: Semiotext(e), p318

[8] Berardi, Franco. (2015). *AND: Phenomenology of the End.* South Pasadena, CA: Semiotext(e), p338

Chapter Fourteen

[1] Cited in Rose, S. (2018/1994). *Nihilism: The Root of the Revolution of the Modern Age.* Platina, CA, St. Herman of Alaska Brotherhood, p28

[2] Rose, S. (2018/1994). *Nihilism: The Root of the Revolution of the Modern Age.* Platina, CA, St. Herman of Alaska Brotherhood, p109

[3] Rose, S. (2018/1994). *Nihilism: The Root of the Revolution of the Modern Age.* Platina, CA, St. Herman of Alaska Brotherhood, p11

⁴ Rose, S. (2018/1994). *Nihilism: The Root of the Revolution of the Modern Age.* Platina, CA, St. Herman of Alaska Brotherhood, p79

⁵ Han, B.-C. (2017). *Psycho-Politics: Neoliberalism and New Technologies of Power.* London, Verso, p59

⁶ Berardi, F. (2019). *The Second Coming.* Cambridge, Polity Press, p54

⁷ Berardi, F. (2019). *The Second Coming.* Cambridge, Polity Press, p39-40

⁸ Cited in Rose, S. (2018/1994). *Nihilism: The Root of the Revolution of the Modern Age.* Platina, CA, St. Herman of Alaska Brotherhood, p91

Chapter Fifteen

¹ Berardi, F. (2019). *The Second Coming.* Cambridge, Polity Press, p3

² Fromm, E. (1993). *The Art of Being.* London, Constable, p96

³ Aurobindo, S. (2003/1963). *The Future Evolution of Man.* Twin Lakes, Lotus Press, p33

⁴ Fromm, E. (1978). *To Have or To Be.* London, Abacus, p165

⁵ Fromm, E. (1978). *To Have or To Be.* London, Abacus, p20

Beautiful Traitor Books was founded in 2012 as an independent print-on-demand imprint to provide unusual and inspiring books for the discerning reader.

Our books are works that delve into various domains whether it is books for children, science fiction, social affairs, philosophy, theatre plays, or poetry. We have books translated into Spanish, French, Portuguese, Italian, and Hungarian.

All the books we publish seek to explore innovative and creative ideas. Many of them also tell a good story - stories that have different perspectives on life and on the human condition.

Beautiful Traitor Books is not only about offering the reader entertainment. We also seek to offer something that is like a nutrition; something of value that the reader can take away from the book. Good books function on more than one level. Put simply, we thrive on books that have the capacity to *shift* the reader.

Come and join the conversation – find out more at:
www.beautifultraitorbooks.com

www.ingramcontent.com/pod-product-compliance
Lightning Source LLC
Chambersburg PA
CBHW071625080526
44588CB00010B/1275